HAS THE BIBLE BEEN CHANGED?

Muslims all over the world are ignoring the message of the New Testament because their teachers say its text has been corrupted. Yet very few of them have checked to see whether what their teachers say is true. Dan Wickwire is one of few Christians who have studied theology both in Christian and Muslim settings, and has spent countless hours responding to Muslims' objections to the reliability of the Bible. And the case he makes in this book is rock-solid. Learn it and you will be well equipped to help Muslims take seriously the good news found in the New Testament.

David Byle
Chairman of the Bible Correspondence Course in Turkey
(bccturkey.org)

Dan Wickwire has lived in the Middle East most of his adult life and has spent endless hours engaging Muslims in friendly but serious dialogue. He is well informed in both Christian and Islamic theology and has specialized in comparing Qur'anic and Christian texts and listening to the arguments of his Muslim friends and, where possible, answering their questions by explaining what the Bible [and the Quran] actually teaches.

Stuart Briscoe
Minister, Elmbrook Church;
Founder, "Telling the Truth Ministries"

Every page of *Has the Bible Been Changed?* is filled with great information, and the pages that covered difficult questions for Muslims to answer were absolutely amazing and extremely helpful.

Dr. Bill Jones
President of Columbia International University and founder of
Crossover Communications International

HAS THE BIBLE BEEN CHANGED?

THE RELIABILITY OF THE SCRIPTURES ACCORDING TO JEWISH, CHRISTIAN, AND ISLAMIC SOURCES

Dan Wickwire

A.A. liberal arts
Th.B. Bible
M.A. Bible
M.A. linguistics

ANEKO
PRESS

Visit Dan's website: www.danwickwire.com

Has the Bible Been Changed? – Dan Wickwire

Copyright © 2016

First edition published 2011

The New Scofield Reference Bible Authorized King James Version, Oxford University Press, USA, 1967

Verses quoted from the Qur'an are taken from: *The Holy Qur'an With English Translation,* İlmi Neşriyat, İstanbul, Turkey, 1992

Cover Design: Natalia H., BookCoverLabs.com

Cover Photography: Anna Poguliaeva/Shutterstock

eBook Icon: Icons Vector/Shutterstock

Editors: Ruth Z. & Jeremiah Z.

Printed in the United States of America

Aneko Press – *Our Readers Matter*[TM]

www.anekopress.com

Aneko Press, Life Sentence Publishing, and our logos are trademarks of

Life Sentence Publishing, Inc.
203 E. Birch Street
P.O. Box 652
Abbotsford, WI 54405

RELIGION / Islam / Theology

Paperback ISBN: 978-1-62245-348-1

eBook ISBN: 978-1-62245-349-8

10 9 8 7 6 5 4 3 2 1

Available where books are sold

Table of Contents

Introduction 1

Titles Given to the Bible 4

The Canon of Scripture.. 6

The Criteria Used to Determine Which Books Were Canonical 8

Statistics on the Holy Books.. 10

The Inspiration of the Bible.. 12

God's Word Is Eternal and Unchangeable............................ 14

Muhammad Accepted the Bible 16

The Problem of Abrogation... 18

The Qur'an Says "Verbal Distortion," Not "Corruption" 20

According to the Bible, God's Word Cannot Be Changed 22

According to the Qur'an, God's Word Cannot Be Changed............ 24

No Distinctions Are Allowed Between the Holy Books................... 26

Rejecters of Any of the Holy Books Will Be Punished in Hell........ 28

The Bible Could Not Have Been Changed Before Muhammad 30

The Bible Could Not Have Been Changed After Muhammad 32

Qur'an Verses That Confirm Bible Legitimacy................................ 34

The Qur'an's Critique of Jews and Christians 36

What is the Purpose of God in Relation to His Holy Books?.......... 38

What is the Power of God in Relation to His Holy Books? 40

Fundamental Errors of Logic Which Muslims Make 42

A Correct Logical Syllogism in Relation to the Word of God......... 44

Did God Not Know? 46

Did God Not Care? 48

Could God Not Stop the Changes? 50

Is God Not Faithful?...52

Is God Not Righteous?...54

Is God Not Merciful? 56

Did Satan Win the Battle for the Bible?..58

The Hypocritical Nature of the Claim That the Bible Has Been
    Changed...60

The Detailed Care Taken in Copying the Old Testament 62

Textual Manuscript Evidence for the Holy Books 64

Bible Textual Agreement and Uniformity...66

The Degree of Textual Agreement and Uniformity in the
    Ancient Manuscripts...68

The Patristics (Early Church Fathers)..70

The Cardinal Doctrines of Christ..72

What Happened at the Early Church Councils? 74

What Are the Apocryphal Books?..76

What Is the Gospel of Barnabas?...78

Would the Unfaithfulness of the Jews Affect God's Faithfulness? ..80

What Are the Real Reasons for the Muslim Claims of Corruption?....82

Some Difficult Questions for Muslims to Consider..........................84

Seven Reasons Why Christians Do Not Believe in the Qur'an 86

God's Eternal Plan of Salvation...88

Blessing or Cursing: The Choice Is Yours...94

Index of Biblical Verses 96

Index of Qur'anic Verses..99

Index of Foreign Words Used 102

Bibliography...105

Meet the Author...107

Introduction

Having served as an open church-planting missionary in Turkey and the Middle East for more than thirty years, one of the most frequent issues that I have come across in religious dialogue with Muslims is the Muslim claim that "the Bible has been changed." Young children growing up in the Middle East have been taught in mandatory religious education classes that Jews and Christians have changed and corrupted their own Holy Book, the Bible. For this reason, very few Muslims have ever had the desire to read or study the Bible, even though the Qur'an actually does validate the Bible as being the Word of God.

In 1995, I had the rare privilege of becoming a doctoral student at Ankara University in the Department of Islamic Theology. It was the first time in the history of this Islamic University that they had ever accepted a Christian into this doctoral program. Against all the odds and a good deal of opposition, I was accepted as a special guest student on an auditing basis. I went through the entire doctoral program, and ended up writing a 420-page doctoral thesis in Turkish entitled "Yahudi, Hıristiyan ve İslâm Kaynaklarına göre Kutsal Kitab'ın Değişmezliği" (The Reliability of the Scriptures According to Jewish, Christian, and Islamic Sources.) This book was published in Turkey in 1999, and copies were sent to all the Islamic theological faculties in Turkey – one copy to the rector of each of the Islamic faculties and one copy to each of their libraries. This book liberally quotes as much from the Qur'an as it does from the Bible. Rectors from many of the theological schools in Turkey wrote me letters of appreciation for the book. One of the most prominent theologians in Turkey, a prolific author who also translated the Qur'an into Turkish, Dr. Yaşar Nuri Öztürk, who was then rector of the theological faculty at Marmara University in Istanbul, wrote a review of my book in a Turkish newspaper, where he highly recommended reading this sizable book for anyone who was interested in this subject.

Copies of the book were also distributed to many of the department heads of the theological faculty at Ankara University. One of the professors who read the book was the department head of Islamic philosophy, and was also one of twelve people who sit at the top of the Department of Religious Affairs, which runs all of the mosques in Turkey and controls what students are taught in the mandatory religious education classes for children in the public schools in Turkey. After reading the book, the distinguished professor thanked me and said, "Dan, I have changed my doctrine. I will never again say that the Bible has been changed." A short time later, a decision came down from the Department of Religious Affairs ordering that all of the textbooks used for religious education in Turkey, which had previously been saying that the Bible had been changed, should be withdrawn from the schools and that this section on Christianity should be rewritten. Two professors on the Ankara University theological faculty were commissioned by the Department of Religious Affairs to rewrite these sections. After rewriting the sections on Christianity, both of these professors asked me to review and critique their newly written manuscripts for any errors in content. They accepted all of my suggestions and I accepted their final revisions.

The book which you have in hand, *Has the Bible Been Changed?* is a shortened and simplified version of the original thesis, and this shorter version has been published four times in Turkish and three times in English. I want to express my thanks to the faculty of Ankara University, Department of

Islamic Theology, as I highly value the good memories I have of studying the Qur'an under these able scholars whom I count as my friends. Although there are many things on which we disagree, there are certainly many things about which we can come to mutual agreement. Concerning the Word of God, I can wholeheartedly agree with the Qur'an when it correctly says, "Say: O People of the Scripture! You have nothing (of true guidance) till you <u>observe the Torah and the Gospel</u>, and <u>that which was revealed to you from your Lord</u>." (Mâ'ide 5:68) "Perfected is the Word of your Lord in truth and justice. <u>There is nothing that can change His words</u>." (En'am 6:115)

  – Dan Wickwire

Titles Given to the Bible

In the Bible

The **Scriptures** .... Matthew 22:29

The **Holy Scriptures** .... Romans 1:2

The **Old Testament** .... 2 Corinthians 3:14

The **New Testament** .... 2 Corinthians 3:6

The **Writings** .... John 5:47

The **Word of God** .... Hebrews 4:12

The **Word** .... James 1:21-23

The **Word of Life** .... Philippians 2:16

The **Book of the Law** .... Nehemiah 8:3

The **Law of the Lord** .... Psalm 1:2

The **Books of the Prophets** .... Luke 4:17

1 Samuel 9:9 – Beforetime in Israel, when a man went to enquire of God, thus he spake, Come, and let us go to the seer: for <u>he that is now called a Prophet</u>[1] <u>was beforetime called a Seer.</u>

John 4:29 – Come, <u>see a man, which told me all things that ever I did</u>: is not this the Christ?

Revelation 19:10 – The testimony of Jesus is the <u>spirit of prophecy</u>.

---

1   In the Bible a "prophet" (*nebi*) is defined as a "seer" i.e. one who can see into the future by the prophetic gift of God. There are 8,362 prophetic verses in the Bible which means that about 26% of the Bible was prophetic in nature at the time it was written.

In the Qur'an

The Scripture... Al-i İmran 3:3

Allah's Book .... Al-i İmran 3:23

The Word of Allah .... Bakara 2:75

The Revelations of Allah............................. Al-i İmran 3:113

The Revelations of the Compassionate God ... Meryem 19:58

The Criterion (between right and wrong) .... Bakara 2:48

A Light and Reminder .... Enbiyâ 21:48

The Reminder .... Enbiyâ 21:7

A Guidance and a Light .... Mâ'ide 5:44, 46

While over a quarter of the verses in the Bible are prophetic in nature, it is evident that the Qur'an does not contain any verses at all which are written in a prophetic genre. The Qur'an itself admits to the fact that Muhammad was not given any prophetic gift whatsoever.

En'âm 6:50 – Say (O Muhammad), to the disbelievers: "I say not to you (that) I possess the treasures of Allah, nor that I have knowledge of the Unseen ... I follow only that which is inspired in me."

A'raf 7:188 – Had I knowledge of the Unseen, I should have abundance of wealth, and adversity would not touch me. I am but a warner, and a bearer of glad tidings unto a people who believe.

Ahkâf 46:9 – Say to them: "I am no new thing among the Messengers. I do not know what shall befall you tomorrow or what shall befall me."

The Canon of Scripture

The 39 Books of the Old Testament[1] (*Tanakh*)

Pentateuch: (*Torah*) x 5

Genesis .... 1446 BC

Exodus .... 1406 BC

Leviticus................... 1490 BC

Numbers.................. 1490 BC

Deuteronomy .... 1451 BC

Poetry: (*Kethubim*) x 13

Psalms .... 1000 BC

Proverbs .... 971 BC

Job .... 1520 BC

Song of Solomon ..... 1014 BC

Ruth .... 1322 BC

Lamentations .... 588 BC

Ecclesiastes .... 977 BC

Esther.......................... 521 BC

Daniel .... 607 BC

Ezra .... 536 BC

Nehemiah................... 446 BC

1 Chronicles .... 1004 BC

2 Chronicles ....1015 BC

Prophets: (*Nebi'im*) x 21

Joshua .... 1451 BC

Judges .... 1425 BC

1 Samuel....................1171 BC

2 Samuel.................... 1056 BC

1 Kings......................1015 BC

2 Kings....................... 896 BC

Isaiah .... 760 BC

Jeremiah..................... 629 BC

Ezekiel .... 595 BC

Hosea .... 785 BC

Joel............................. 800 BC

Amos........................... 787 BC

Obadiah .... 587 BC

Jonah.......................... 862 BC

Micah......................... 750 BC

Nahum........................ 713 BC

Habakkuk.................. 626 BC

Zephaniah.................. 630 BC

Haggai .... 520 BC

Zechariah................... 520 BC

Malachi...................... 425 BC

---

1   Dating statistics compiled from Dake, Robinson & Slick.

The 27 Books of the New Testament[1]

Gospels: *(Injil)* x 4

Matthew .... AD 60

Mark............................ AD 58

Luke ....AD 61

John............................. AD 90

Historical: x 1

Acts .... AD 63

Pauline Epistles: x 13

Romans .... AD 57

1 Corinthians............. AD 54

2 Corinthians............. AD 56

Galatians..................... AD 48

Ephesians.................... AD 60

Philippians .... AD 54

Colossians................... AD 60

1 Thessalonians .... AD 50

2 Thessalonians .... AD 50

1 Timothy .... AD 63

2 Timothy .... AD 63

Titus............................ AD 63

Philemon..................... AD 60

General Epistles: x 8

Hebrews....................... AD 69

James........................... AD 69

1 Peter......................... AD 63

2 Peter......................... AD 64

1 John.......................... AD 90

2 John.......................... AD 90

3 John.......................... AD 90

Jude .... AD 90

Eschatological: x 1

Revelation .... AD 95

---

1   Dating statistics compiled from Dake, Robinson & Slick.

The Criteria Used to Determine Which Books Were Canonical

From the writings of biblical and church history, we can discern at least five principles that guided the recognition and collection of true divinely inspired books. McDowell gives a summary of Geisler & Nix[1] (GIB 223-231), which outlines the criteria that was used for New Testament canonicity which may be summarized as follows:

1) **Apostolicity**: Was it written by a recognized prophet, apostle, or disciple of Jesus or a close associate of a disciple? If it was written by a spokesman for God, then it was the Word of God.

2) **Consistency**: Are the writings in harmony with the other parts of Scripture? Are they truthful and accurate? Did they tell the truth about God? If anything was found in a writing that was not true, it would be dismissed as not from God. God Himself said in Deuteronomy 18:20-22 that if a prophet claims to be speaking from God, and what he said is not true, then he has not spoken from God. God cannot contradict Himself (2 Corinthians 1:17-18), nor can He utter what is false (Hebrews 6:18). For reasons such as these, the church fathers maintained the policy: "If in doubt, throw it out."

3) **Recognition**: Were the writings universally recognized and accepted by the churches? Were they accepted by the people of God? Paul said of the Thessalonians, *For this reason we also constantly thank God that when you received the word of God which you heard from us, you accepted it not as the word of men, but for what it really is, the word of God* (1 Thessalonians 2:13). When a book was received, collected, read, and used by the

---

1   Geisler & Nix, *A General Introduction to the Bible*, pp. 223-231.

people of God as the Word of God, it was regarded as canonical. The apostle Peter acknowledges Paul's writings as Scripture on par with the Old Testament Scripture (2 Peter 3:16).

4) **Inspiration**: Does the book contain evidences of the fact that it is the inspired Word of God? Does it come with the power of God? The church fathers believed the Word of God is *living and active* (Hebrews 4:12) and consequently ought to be a transforming force for edification (2 Timothy 3:17) and evangelization (1 Peter 1:25).

5) **Miracles**: Was the writer confirmed by acts of God? Frequently, miracles separated the true prophets from the false ones. Moses was given miraculous powers to prove his call of God (Exodus 4:1-9). Elijah triumphed over the false prophets of Baal by a supernatural act (1 Kings 18:19-38). Jesus was *approved by God among you by miracles and wonders and signs, which God did by him* (Acts 2:22).

Recognition of the New Testament by the Early Church Fathers[1]

Athanasius: (AD 293-373) The patriarch of Alexandria was the first person to identify the twenty-seven books of the New Testament that are in use today in an Easter letter in AD 327. He is known as the father of the canon.

Jerome: (347-420) Shortly after Athanasius circulated his list of the canonical books, Jerome agreed with this and defined the New Testament canon of twenty-seven books.

Augustine: (354-430) He agreed with Athanasius and Jerome concerning the twenty-seven books of the New Testament.

Pope Damasus I: (305-384) This bishop of Rome used the same list of twenty-seven books as Athanasius in AD 327.

1   McDowell, *The New Evidence*, pp. 23-24.

Statistics on the Holy Books

The Old Testament = 39 books

Books	Chapters	Verses	Words	Letters
39	929	23,138	602,582	2,728,100

The New Testament = 27 books

Books	Chapters	Verses	Words	Letters
27	260	7,957	180,552	838,380

The Bible as a Whole[1] = 66 books

Books	Chapters	Verses	Words	Letters
66	1,189	31,101	783,137	3,566,480

As Compared With the Qur'an[2]

Books	Chapters	Verses	Words	Letters
1	114	6,236	77,934	326,048

When word and letter counts are compared between the Qur'an and the Bible as a whole, of the Holy Books which Muslims are required to believe in (namely, the *Tevrat, Zebur, İnjil,* and Qur'an[3]), the Bible makes up over 90 percent of the content of the Holy Books which Muslims are required to believe in.

In light of the fact that an exact count for the very words and letters used in all of the Holy Books is readily available for both the Bible and the Qur'an, it is obvious that those Holy Books could not be changed without the word and letter count being changed as well. The fact that these numbers are fixed and well known is a testimony to the fact that the Holy Books have not been changed.

---

1   Andrew E. Hill, *Baker's Handbook of Bible Lists*, 1981.
    Finis Jennings Dake, *Dake Annotated Reference Bible*, 1981.
    Note: The statistics used above for the Bible are taken from The King James Version.
2   Osman Keskioğlu, *Nûzulünden İtibaren Kur'an-ı Kerim*, pp. 124-125.
3   For the books which Muslims are required to believe, see 16 &26-28.

The Chronological Order and Dating of the Suras[1]

Sura	Ref	Sura	Ref	Sura	Ref
1. Fatiha	#5. Mekke-1	39. Zümer	#59. Mekke-2	77. Mürselât	#33. Mekke-1
2. Bakara	#87. Medine-4	40. Mümin	#60. Mekke-2	78. Nebe'	#80. Mekke-1
3. Al-i İmran	#89. Medine-5	41. Fussilet	#61. Mekke-2	79. Naziât	#81. Mekke-1
4. Nisâ	#92. Medine-6	42. Şûrâ	#62. Mekke-2	80. Abese	#24. Mekke-1
5. Mâ'ide	#112. Medine-6	43. Zuhruf	#63. Mekke-2	81. Tekvir	#7. Mekke-1
6. En'âm	#55. Mekke-3	44. Duhân	#64. Mekke-2	82. İnfitâr	#82. Mekke-1
7. A'râf	#39. Mekke-3	45. Câsiye	#65. Mekke-2	83. Mutaffifîn	#86. Mekke-1
8. Enfâl	#88. Medine-4	46. Ahkâf	#66. Mekke-2	84. Inşikak	#83. Mekke-1
9. Tevbe	#113. Medine-7	47. Muhammad	#95. Medine-4	85. Bürûc	#27. Mekke-1
10. Yûnus	#51. Mekke-3	48. Fetih	#111. Medine-6	86. Târık	#36. Mekke-1
11. Hûd	#52. Mekke-3	49. Hucurât	#106. Medine-7	87. A'lâ	#8. Mekke-1
12. Yûsuf	#53. Mekke-3	50. Kâf	#34. Mekke-1	88. Gaşiye	#68. Mekke-1
13. R'ad	#96. Mekke-3	51. Zâriyât	#67. Mekke-1	89. Fecr	#10. Mekke-1
14. İbrahim	#72. Mekke-3	52. Tûr	#76. Mekke-1	90. Beled	#35. Mekke-1
15. Hicr	#54. Mekke-3	53. Necm	#23. Mekke-1	91. Şems	#26. Mekke-1
16. Nahl	#70. Mekke-3	54. Kamer	#37. Mekke-1	92. Leyl	#9. Mekke-1
17. Isrâ	#50. Mekke-1	55. Rahmân	#97. Mekke-1	93. Duhâ	#11. Mekke-1
18. Kehf	#69. Mekke-1	56. Vâkıa	#46. Mekke-1	94. Inşirâh	#12. Mekke-1
19. Meryem	#44. Mekke-1	57. Hadîd	#94. Medine-6	95. Tîn	#28. Mekke-1
20. Tâhâ	#45. Mekke-1	58. Mücâdele	#105. Medine-5	96. Alâk	#1. Mekke-1
21. Enbiyâ	#73. Mekke-1	59. Haşr	#101. Medine-5	97. Kadir	#25. Mekke-1
22. Hac	#103. Mekke-3	60. Mümtehine	#91. Medine-6	98. Beyyine	#100. Mekke-1
23. Mü'minûn	#74. Mekke-3	61. Saf	#109. Medine-4	99. Zelzele	#93. Mekke-1
24. Nûr	#102. Medine-6	62. Cum'a	#110. Medine-4	100. Âdiyât	#14. Mekke-1
25. Furkan	#42. Mekke-3	63. Münâfikun	#104. Medine-6	101. Kaari'a	#30. Mekke-1
26. Şuarâ	#47. Mekke-3	64. Teğâbun	#108. Medine-4	102. Tekâsür	#16. Mekke-1
27. Neml	#48. Mekke-3	65. Talâk	#99. Medine-6	103. Asr	#13. Mekke-1
28. Kasas	#49. Mekke-3	66. Tahrîm	#107. Medine-7	104. Hümeze	#32. Mekke-1
29. Ankebut	#85. Mekke-2	67. Mülk	#77. Mekke-1	105. Fîl	#19. Mekke-1
30. Rum	#84. Mekke-2	68. Kalem	#2. Mekke-1	106. Kureyş	#29. Mekke-1
31. Lokman	#57. Mekke-2	69. Hâkka	#78. Mekke-1	107. Mâ'ûn	#17. Mekke-1
32. Secde	#75. Mekke-2	70. Meâric	#79. Mekke-1	108. Kevser	#15. Mekke-1
33. Ahzâb	#90. Medine-6	71. Nûh	#71. Mekke-1	109. Kâfirûn	#18. Mekke-1
34. Sebe'	#58. Mekke-2	72. Cin	#40. Mekke-1	110. Nasr	#114. Medine-7
35. Fâtır	#43. Mekke-2	73. Müzzemmil	#3. Mekke-1	111. Tebbet	#6. Mekke-1
36. Yâsin	#41. Mekke-2	74. Müddessir	#4. Mekke-1	112. İhlâs	#22. Mekke-1
37. Sâffât	#56. Mekke-2	75. Kıyâmet	#31. Mekke-1	113. Felâk	#20. Mekke-1
38. Sâd	#38. Mekke-2	76. İnsan	#98. Mekke-1	114. Nâs	#21. Mekke-1

---

1 Keskioğlu, *Nûzulünden İtibaren Kur'an-ı Kerim*, pp. 124-125.
See 18 for the chronological breakdown of the Mecca and Medina suras.

The Inspiration of the Bible

1 Corinthians 14:37-38 – (37) If any man think himself to be a prophet, or spiritual, let him acknowledge that <u>the things that I write unto you are the commandments of the Lord</u>. (38) But if any man be ignorant, let him be ignorant.

Galatians 1:11-12 – (11) But I [make known to] you, brethren, that <u>the gospel</u> which was preached [by] me is not after man. (12) For I neither received it of man, neither was I taught it, but <u>by the revelation of Jesus Christ</u>.

2 Timothy 3:14-17 – (14) But continue thou in the things which thou hast learned and hast been assured of, knowing of whom thou hast learned them; (15) and that from a child thou hast known <u>the holy scriptures</u>, which are able to make thee wise unto salvation through faith which is in Jesus Christ. (16) <u>All scripture is given by inspiration of God</u>, and is profitable for doctrine, for reproof, for correction, for instruction in righteousness: (17) that the man of God may be perfect, thoroughly furnished unto all good works.

2 Peter 1:20-21 – (20) Knowing this first, that no prophecy of <u>the scripture</u> is of any private interpretation. (21) For the prophecy came not at any time by the will of man: but <u>holy men of God spake as they were moved by the Holy Ghost</u>.

Revelation 1:1-3 – (1) <u>The Revelation of Jesus Christ, which God gave unto him</u>, to shew unto his servants things which must shortly come to pass; and he sent and signified it by his angel unto his servant John: (2) who bare record of <u>the word of God</u>, and of the testimony of Jesus Christ, and of all things that he saw. (3) <u>Blessed is he that readeth, and they that hear the words of this prophecy, and keep those things which are written therein</u>: for the time is at hand.

1. The Bible was written by approximately forty authors over a period of sixteen hundred years and by different types of people in different parts of the world.

2. The Old Testament was originally written in Hebrew, with parts of Daniel and Ezra being written in Aramaic. The New Testament was written in Greek.

3. Its subject matter includes hundreds of controversial subjects, yet there is a harmony and unity throughout, such that any part of the Bible can only be explained accurately in reference to the whole.

4. The continuity of the message of the Bible is absolute in its completeness. It is bound together by historical sequence, type and anti-type, prophecy and its fulfillment, and by the anticipation, presentation, realization, and exaltation of the most perfect Person who ever walked the earth and whose glories are the radiance of heaven. Yet the perfection of this continuity is sustained against what to man would be insurmountable impediments; for the Bible is a collection of sixty-six books which have been written by over forty different authors – kings, peasants, philosophers, fishermen, physicians, statesmen, scholars, poets, and plowmen – who lived their lives in various countries and experienced no conference or agreement with one another, and over a period of not less than sixteen hundred years of human history. Because of these obstacles to continuity, the Bible would naturally be the most heterogeneous, incommensurable, inconsonant, and contradictory collection of human opinions the world has ever seen; but on the contrary, it is just what it is designed to be, namely, a homogeneous, uninterrupted, harmonious, and orderly account of the whole history of God's dealings with man. The Bible is not such a book a man would write if he could, or could write if he would.[1]

---

1   Lewis Sperry Chafer, *Systematic Theology*, Vol. 1, p. 29

God's Word Is Eternal and Unchangeable

According to the Bible

Psalm 33:11 – The counsel of the LORD <u>standeth for ever</u>, the thoughts of his heart <u>to all generations</u>.

Psalm 111:7-8 – (7) The works of his hands are verity and justice; <u>all his commandments are sure.</u> (8) They <u>stand fast for ever and ever.</u>

Psalm 119:152 – Concerning <u>thy testimonies</u>, I have known of old that <u>thou hast founded them for ever.</u>

Psalm 119:160 – Thy word is true from the beginning: and <u>every one of thy righteous judgments endureth for ever.</u>

Matthew 28:20 – Teaching them to <u>observe all things whatsoever I have commanded you</u>; and, lo, <u>I am with you always, even unto the end of the world.</u>

Luke 21:33 – Heaven and earth shall pass away: but <u>my words shall not pass away.</u>

Hebrews 4:12 – For <u>the word of God is [living], and powerful,</u> and sharper than any twoedged sword.

Hebrews 13:8 – <u>Jesus Christ the same yesterday, and to day, and for ever.</u>

1 Peter 1:23, 25 – (23) Being born again, not of corruptible seed, but of <u>incorruptible</u>, by <u>the word of God, which liveth and abideth forever</u>. (25) But <u>the word of the Lord endureth for ever.</u>

According to the Qur'an

Al-i İmran 3:39 – Allah gives you the glad tidings of a son whose name is John, who comes to confirm a <u>word from Allah</u>, princely and chaste, a Prophet of the righteous.

> **Note:** "word" = *Kalimullah* in Arabic. John as a prophet was sent to confirm Jesus, who is the eternal and unchangeable "word" (*logos*) from Allah.

Al-i İmran 3:45, 55 – (45) Allah gives glad tidings of a <u>word from Him</u>, whose name is Messiah, Jesus ... one who shall be brought near to God ... (55) Allah said to Jesus! I am ... setting those who follow you above those who disbelieve until the day of Resurrection.

Nisâ 4:171 – The Messiah son of Mary, was only a messenger of Allah, and <u>His word</u> which He conveyed to Mary and a spirit from Him.

Zuhruf 43:4 – verily it is inscribed in <u>the mother of the Book</u>, which We possess ...

> **Note**: "<u>The Mother of the Book</u>' (*Levh-i Mahfuz*) is the original tablet preserved in Heaven from which all the Books revealed to the prophets have been derived." (Footnote for Zuhruf 43:4 in *The Holy Qur'an*, "İlmi Neşriyat, p. 488.)

Hadîd 57:22 – No misfortune can befall in the earth, or your own persons, but it is recorded in a <u>book</u> before We bring it into being. That is easy for Allah.

> **Note:** "book" = *Levh-i Mahfuz*, cf. 85:22.

Muhammad Accepted the Bible

According to the Qur'an, Muhammad accepted the Bible that existed at his time as the Word of God:

Bakara 2:136 – Say (O Muslims): <u>We believe in</u> Allah and <u>that which is revealed to</u> us, and that which is revealed to Abraham, Ishmael, Isaac, Jacob, and the tribes; to <u>Moses and Jesus and the (other) prophets by their Lord</u>.

Al-i İmran 3:3 – He has revealed to you (Muhammad) the Scripture with truth, <u>confirming that which was revealed before it</u>, even as He revealed the <u>Torah</u> and the <u>Gospel</u>.

Al-i İmran 3:119 – <u>you believe in all the Scripture</u>.

Nisâ 4:136 – O you who believe! <u>Believe in</u> Allah and His messenger and the Scripture which he has revealed to His messenger and <u>the Scripture which He revealed before you</u>.

Mâ'ide 5:46 – We sent <u>Jesus</u> son of Mary, <u>confirming that which was (revealed) before him</u>, and <u>We bestowed on him the Gospel wherein is guidance and a light</u>, conforming that which was (revealed) before it in <u>the Torah – a guidance and an admonition to the God-fearing</u>.

Mâ'ide 5:68 – Say: "O People of the Scripture! You have nothing (of true guidance) till you <u>observe the Torah and the Gospel</u>, and <u>that which was revealed to you from your Lord</u>."

Tevbe 9:111 – That is <u>a promise binding upon Allah in the Torah and the Gospel</u> and the Qur'an.

İsra 17:55 – And We preferred some of the prophets above others; and <u>unto David We gave the Psalms</u>.

Ankebut 29:46 – Say: <u>We believe in that which was revealed unto you</u>; our God and your God is One.

Sejde 32:23 – We verily gave Moses the Book; so be not you in doubt of his receiving it; and We appointed it a guidance for the Children of İsrael.

Fussilat 41:43 – O Prophet, nothing is said to you that has not already been said to the Messengers before you.

Shu'ara 42:15 – Therefore, (O Muhammad) call them (to the true faith), and hold fast to it yourself as you have been commanded, and do not follow their whims, but say: "I believe in whatever Book Allah has sent down ..."

Zuhruf 43:61, 63 – (61) And (the second coming of Jesus shall be) a sign of the Hour: therefore, do not have any doubt about it, and follow Me. This is the Straight Way.... (63) And when Jesus came with clear proofs he said ... fear Allah and obey me.

Ahkâf 46:12 – Yet before it there came the Book of Moses as a guide and a mercy; and this book has been revealed to confirm it in the Arabic language so as to warn the wrongdoers and to give good news to those who do good.

Hadîd 57:27 – Then We caused Our messengers to follow in their footsteps; and We caused Jesus, son of Mary, to follow, and gave him the Gospel, and placed compassion and mercy in the hearts of those who followed him.

The Problem of Abrogation

According to the Bible

Psalm 89:34 – My covenant will I not break, <u>nor alter the thing that is gone out of my lips.</u>

Psalm 105:7-8, 10 – (7) He is the LORD our God: his judgments are in all the earth. (8) He hath <u>remembered his covenant for ever</u>, the word which he commanded to a <u>thousand generations</u>. (10) … an <u>everlasting covenant</u>.

Malachi 3:6 – For <u>I am the LORD</u>, <u>I change not</u>.

Matthew 5:17-18 – (17) <u>Think not that I am come to destroy the law, or the prophets</u>: I am not come to destroy, but to fulfil. (18) For verily I say unto you, <u>Till heaven and earth pass, one jot or one tittle shall in no way pass from the law</u>, till all be fulfilled.

Luke 16:17 – And <u>it is easier for heaven and earth to pass, than one tittle of the law to fail</u>.

James 1:17 – Every good gift and every perfect gift is from above, and cometh down from the <u>Father of lights, with whom is no variableness, neither shadow of turning</u>.

> **Note**: The law of abrogation in the Bible applies only to the New Testament fulfilling the prophecies of the Old Testament and thus completing and superseding them. (cf. Jeremiah 31:31-34; Hebrews 7:18, 22; Hebrews 8:13; Hebrews 9:14-26; Hebrews 10:9-10; Colossians 2:14; 2 Corinthians 3:4-6, 9-11; Galatians 4:8-11; Galatians 5:1, 6, 18; Galatians 6:15; Ephesians 2:14-15).

According to the Qur'an

Bakara 2:106 – <u>If we abrogate any verse or cause it to be forgotten</u>, We replace it by a better or a similar one.

Ra'd 13:39 – <u>Allah blots out or confirms whatever He will</u>, and with Him is the Mother of the Book.

Nahl 16:101 – <u>When we exchange a revelation in place of another revelation</u> – and Allah know best what He reveals – they say: "You are an imposter." Indeed, most of them have no knowledge.

İsra 17:86 – And <u>if We had willed We could certainly take away that which We have revealed to you;</u>

> **Note:** The law of abrogation within Islam (*nesih* or *mensuh*) commonly <u>applies only to the verses of the Qur'an within itself</u>. However, among Muslim scholars there is no agreement as to which verses of the Qur'an abrogate which, but it is roughly based upon an estimated chronological dating of the suras, the later verses said to abrogate the verses which were written earlier. The chronological timetable of the twenty-three years for the writing of the suras of the Qur'an may be divided into seven periods:[1]

at Mecca - 1	1st to 5th year	612-617	= 60 suras
at Mecca - 2	6th to 10th year	617-619	= 17 suras
at Mecca - 3	11th to 13th year	619-622	= 15 suras
at Medina - 4	14th to 15th year	623-624	= 6 suras
at Medina - 5	16th to 17th year	625-626	= 3 suras
at Medina - 6	18th to 21st year	627-630	= 9 suras
at Medina - 7	22nd to 23rd year	631-632	= 4 suras

---

1   Keskioğlu, *Nûzulünden İtibaren Kur'an-ı Kerim*, pp. 124-125.
(See 11 for the time period of each sura.)

The Qur'an Says "Verbal Distortion," Not "Corruption"

The Qur'an does not speak of any corruption the text of the Bible (*Tahrif bil Lafız*) but it does speak of a verbal distortion of its meaning (*Tahrif bil Mana*).

Bakara 2:75 – Now (O company of believers), do you then hope that they will believe in you, when some of them have already heard the word of Allah and knowingly perverted it, after they had understood its meaning?

Al-i İmran 3:78 – And there is a party of them who distort the Scriptures with their tongues, that you may think that what they say is from the Scripture, when it is not from the Scripture. And they say: "It is from Allah," when it is not from Allah, and they speak a lie concerning Allah knowingly.

Nisâ 4:46 – Some of those who are Jews change words from their context and say: "We hear and disobey; hear you as one who hears not"; and "listen to us!" distorting with their tongues and belittling religion.

Mâ'ide 5:13 – And because of their breaking their covenant, We have cursed them and made hard their hearts. They change words from their context and forget a part of that wherewith they had been reminded.

Mâ'ide 5:41 – "O Messenger! Do not be grieved by those who vie with one another in the race to disbelief, of such as say with their mouths: 'We believe,' but their hearts believe not, and of the Jews: listeners for the sake of falsehood, listeners on behalf of other people who come not to you, changing words from their context and saying: 'If this be given to you, receive it, but if this be not given to you, then beware!'"

En'âm 6:91 – And they measure not the power of Allah its true measure when they say: "Allah has revealed nothing to a human being." Say (to the Jews who speak thus): "Who revealed the book which Moses brought, a light and guidance for mankind, which you have put on parchments which you show, but you hide much (thereof), and by which you were taught that which you knew not yourselves nor did your fathers (know it)?" Say: "Allah." Then leave them to their plunge into their games.

A'raf 7:162 – But those of them who did wrong changed the word which had been told them for another saying, and We sent down upon them wrath from heaven for their wrongdoing.

A'raf 7:157 – Those who follow the messenger, the prophet who can neither read nor write, whom they find described in the Torah and Gospel which are with them ...

Saf 61:6-7 – (6) And remember Jesus, son of Mary, who said: "O Children of İsrael; I am the messenger of Allah to you, confirming that which was revealed before me in the Torah (Books of Moses) and bringing good tidings of a messenger who will come after me, whose name is Ahmad."[1] Yet when he has come to them with clear proofs, they say: "This is mere magic." (7) And who is more wicked than the man who invents a falsehood about Allah when called to Islam. Allah does not guide the wrongdoers.

---

1   "Muhammad (Ahmad being one of his names)" *The Holy Qur'an*, "İlmi Neşriyat, p. 551.

According to the Bible, God's Word Cannot Be Changed

The Pentateuch *(Torah)*

Genesis 17:7, 19 – (7) And I will establish <u>my covenant</u> between me and thee and thy seed after thee <u>in their generations for an everlasting covenant</u>, to be a God unto thee, and to thy seed after thee. (19) And God said, Sarah thy wife shall bear thee a son indeed; and thou shalt call his name Isaac: and <u>I will establish my covenant with him for an everlasting covenant, and with his seed after him</u>.

Deuteronomy 7:9 – Know therefore that the Lord thy God, he is <u>God, the faithful God, who keepeth covenant and mercy with them that love him and keep his commandments to a thousand generations</u>.

Deuteronomy 29:29 – The secret things belong unto the Lord our God: but <u>those things which are revealed belong unto us and to our children forever</u>, that we may do all the words of this law.

The Psalms *(Kethubim)*

Psalm 89:31, 34 – (31) If they break my statutes, and keep not my commandments; (34) My covenant will I not break, nor alter the thing that is gone out of my lips.

Psalm 119:160 – Thy word is true from the beginning: and <u>every one of thy righteous judgments endureth for ever</u>.

Psalm 119:89-90 – (89) <u>For ever</u>, O Lord, <u>thy word is settled in heaven</u>. (90) <u>Thy faithfulness is unto all generations</u>.

The Prophets *(Nebi'im)*

2 Samuel 7:24-25 – (24) For thou hast <u>confirmed</u> to thyself thy people İsrael to be a people unto thee <u>for ever</u>: and thou, LORD, art become their God. (25) And now, O LORD God, <u>the word that thou hast spoken</u> concerning thy servant, and concerning his house, <u>establish it for ever</u>, and do <u>as thou hast said</u>.

Isaiah 40:8 – The grass withereth, the flower fadeth, but <u>the word of our God shall stand for ever</u>.

Isaiah 55:11 – So shall <u>my word</u> be that goeth forth out of my mouth: <u>it shall not return unto me void</u>, but <u>it shall accomplish that which I please</u>, and <u>it shall prosper</u> in the thing whereto I sent it.

The New Testament *(İnjil)*

Matthew 5:18 – Till heaven and earth pass, one jot or <u>one tittle shall in no wise pass from the law</u>, till all be fulfilled.

Matthew 24:35 – Heaven and earth shall pass away, but <u>my words shall not pass away</u>.

1 Peter 1:23, 25 – (23) Being born again, not of corruptible seed, but of <u>incorruptible</u>, by <u>the word of God which liveth and abideth for ever</u>. (25) But <u>the word of the Lord endureth for ever</u>.

Revelation 14:6 – And I saw another angel fly in the midst of heaven, having <u>the everlasting gospel</u> to preach unto them that dwell in the earth.

According to the Qur'an, God's Word Cannot Be Changed

En'âm 6:34 – <u>There is none to alter the decisions of Allah.</u>

En'âm 6:115 – Perfected is the Word of your Lord in truth and justice. <u>There is nothing that can change His words.</u>

Yunus 10:64 – <u>No change can there be in the words of Allah.</u>

İbrahim 14:47 – <u>Never think that Allah will fail in his promise to his messengers.</u>

İsra 17:77 – (Such was Our) way with the messengers We sent before you. And <u>you will find no change in Our ways.</u>

Kehf 18:27 – <u>No one can change His words.</u>

Hajj 22:47, 52 – (47) Allah shall <u>never fail his promise</u> … (52) But <u>Allah abrogates what Satan casts. Then Allah establishes (perfects) His signs (revelations),</u> and Allah is All-Knowing, All-Wise.

Ahzab 33:62 – <u>That was the way</u> of Allah in the case of those who passed away <u>of old; you will not find for the way of Allah any changing.</u>

Fâtir 35:43 – <u>You will not find</u> for Allah's way of treatment <u>any substitute,</u> <u>or</u> will you find for Allah's way to treatment aught of <u>power to change.</u>

Hakka 69:44-47 – (44) And <u>if he had invented false sayings concerning Us,</u> (45) <u>We assuredly had taken him by the right hand</u> (46) <u>and then severed his life-artery,</u> (47) and none of you could have held Us off from him.

Hijr 15:9 – We have, without doubt, sent down <u>the Reminder</u>, and <u>we preserve it</u>.

Nahl 16:43 – The messengers We sent before you (O Muhammad), were not other than men to whom <u>We gave revelation</u>. Ask the people of <u>the Remembrance</u> if you do not know.

Enbiyâ 21:7, 48, 105 – (7) Before you (also), the messengers We sent were only men, to whom We had granted revelation. If you do not know this, ask those who have <u>the Reminder</u>[1] ... (48) We gave Moses and Aaron the Criterion (or right and wrong) and a light and <u>Reminder</u> for those who keep from evil ... (105) And verily We have written in the Zebûr (Scripture) after <u>the reminder</u>: "My righteous slaves shall inherit the earth." (cf. Psalm 37:29)

Mu'min 40:53-54 – And we did give Moses the guidance and made the Children of Israel to inherit <u>the Scripture</u>. A guide and <u>a reminder</u> for men of understanding ...

Fetih 48:23 – This is <u>the way of Allah that has been followed in the past</u>, and <u>you will find no change in the way of Allah</u>.

Kaf 50:29 – <u>My word cannot be changed</u>.

---

1   The word *reminder* that occurs in these verses is usually taken to refer to the Torah. (Footnote taken from Enbiyâ 21:105, *The Holy Qur'an*, "İlmi Neşriyat, p. 330.)

No Distinctions Are Allowed Between the Holy Books

According to the Qur'an, Muslims are not allowed to make any distinctions between the holy books.

Bakara 2:62 – Those who believe (in the Qur'an and <u>the Prophets sent before you</u>), <u>Jews,</u> <u>Christians,</u> and Sabeans; whoever believes in Allah and the Last Day and does what is right; <u>shall be rewarded by their Lord</u>; no fear shall come upon them, neither shall they regret.

Bakara 2:85, 121 – (85) <u>Do you believe in one part of the Scripture and disbelieve in another?</u>... (121) Those to whom we gave the Scripture, and who read it the way it should be read, truly believe in it. And <u>those who deny it are the true losers</u>.

Bakara 2:136 – Say (O Muslims): <u>We believe in</u> Allah and that which is revealed to us, and <u>that which is revealed to</u> Abraham, Ishmael, Isaac, Jacob, and the tribes; to <u>Moses</u> and <u>Jesus and the (other) prophets by their Lord</u>. We make no distinction between any of them, and to Allah we have surrendered ourselves.

Bakara 2:285 – The Messenger believes in what has been revealed to him by his Lord, and <u>so do the believers</u>. They all believe in Allah and His angels, <u>His Scriptures</u> and <u>His messengers</u>: "<u>We make no distinction between any of His messengers</u>" – and they say: "We <u>hear</u> and <u>obey</u>."

Al-i İmran 3:84 – Say (O Muhammad) "<u>We believe in</u> ... that which was revealed to ... <u>Moses</u> and <u>Jesus</u> and <u>the Prophets</u> from their Lord. We make no distinction between any of them...

Al-i İmran 3:199 – <u>There are certainly among the People of the Scriptures some who believe in</u> Allah and that which is revealed to you and <u>that which was revealed to them</u> humbling themselves before Allah. They will not sell the revelations (signs) of Allah for a miserable price. Verily their reward is in the presence of their Lord.

Nisâ 4:150-151 – (150) Those who disbelieve in Allah and His messengers, and seek to <u>make distinction between Allah and His messengers</u>, and say: "We believe in some and disbelieve in others," and seek to choose a way in between ... (151) Such are <u>disbelievers in truth</u>; and for disbelievers We prepare a humiliating punishment.

Nisâ 4:162 – But those of them who are firm in knowledge, and the believers, <u>believe in that </u>which is revealed to you, and that <u>which was revealed before you</u>, especially the diligent in prayer and those who pay the Zakat, the believers in Allah and the Last Day. To them We shall bestow a great reward.

Mâ'ide 5:66 – If they had observed (practiced) <u>the Torah and the Gospel and that which was revealed to them from their Lord</u>, they would surely have been <u>nourished from above</u> them and from beneath their feet. Among them there are people who are moderate, but many of them are of evil conduct.

Shu'ara 42:15 – say: "<u>I believe in whatever Book Allah has sent down </u>... Let there be no argument between us."

Rejecters of Any of the Holy Books Will Be Punished in Hell

According to the Qur'an, those who reject any of the Holy Books are unbelievers *(Kâfirler)* who will be punished in hell.

Bakara 2:85, 121 – (85) <u>Do you believe in one part of the Scripture and disbelieve in another?</u> Those of you that act thus shall only be rewarded with <u>disgrace</u> in this world, and with the most <u>grievous punishment</u> on the Day of Resurrection. Allah is not unaware of what you do ... (121) Those to whom we gave <u>the Scripture</u>, and who read it the way it should be read, truly believe in it. And <u>those who deny it are the true losers.</u>

Al-i İmran 3:3-4 – (3) He has revealed to you (Muhammad) the Scripture with truth, confirming that which was revealed before it, even as He revealed <u>the Torah and the Gospel.</u> (4) Previously, for a guidance to mankind, and had revealed the Criterion. <u>Those who deny the signs of Allah shall receive a heavy penalty;</u> and Allah is Mighty, Able to Requite.

Al-i İmran 3:55-56 – (55) Allah said <u>to Jesus!</u> I ... am setting those who follow you above those who disbelieve until the day of Resurrection. (56) <u>As for those who disbelieve, I shall punish them with a heavy chastisement in the world and the Hereafter; and they will have no helpers.</u>

Nisâ 4:150-151 – (150) <u>Those who disbelieve in Allah and His messengers,</u> and seek to make a distinction between Allah and His messengers, and <u>say: "We believe in some and disbelieve in others,"</u> and seek to choose a way in between them. (151) <u>Such are disbelievers</u> in truth; and <u>for disbelievers We prepare a humiliating punishment.</u>

Mâ'ide 5:10, 12 – (10) And <u>those who disbelieve and deny Our signs, such are the rightful owners of hell</u> ... (12) Allah made a covenant of old with the Children of Israel ... <u>Whosoever among you disbelieves after this has gone astray from a straight path.</u>

En'âm 6:157 – <u>Who does greater wrong than he who denies the revelations of Allah</u>, and turns away from them? <u>We award to those who turn away from Our revelations a severe penalty</u>...

Ankebut 29:46-47 – (46) Argue not with the People of the Book unless it be in a way that is better ... and say: "We believe in that which was revealed unto us and revealed unto you; our God and your God is One, and unto Him we surrender ..." (47) And <u>none deny Our revelations save the disbelievers</u>.

Sebe' 34:31, 38 – (31) And <u>those who disbelieve</u> say: "We believe not this Qur'an nor <u>in that which was before it</u> ..." (38) And <u>as for those who strive against Our revelations, challenging, they will be brought to the punishment</u>.

Jathiya 45:16, 31, 34 – (16) Before this, We had bestowed on the Children of Israel the Book and the Command and the Prophethood, and provided them with good things, and favored them above (all) peoples ... (31) <u>And as for those who disbelieved</u> (it will be said:) "Were not My Revelations recited to you? ..." (34) It will be said to them: "This day we forget you, even as you forgot the meeting of this your day; and <u>your habitation is the Fire, and there is none to help you</u>."

The Bible Could Not Have Been Changed Before Muhammad

The Bible could not have been changed before the time of Muhammad, because Muhammad himself accepted the Bible as the valid Word of God.

"Both are <u>readers of the Scripture</u>"

Bakara 2:40, 44, 113

Al-i İmran 3:79, 93-94

A'raf 7:169

"Ask those who <u>have been reading</u> the Book before you"

Yunus 10:94-95

Nahl 16:43

İsra 17:101

Ta-Ha 20:133

Enbiyâ 21:7, 10, 105

Zuhruf 43:45-46

"We did reveal <u>the Torah</u> ... <u>a light and a guidance</u>"

Mâ'ide 5:44-45

Ahkâf 46:12

Kasas 28:48-49

Say "O <u>People of the Scripture!</u>"

Al-i İmran 3:64, 65, 69-72, 75

"<u>They have</u> their own law (Torah) <u>wherein Allah delivered judgment</u>"

Bakara 2:41, 91

Nisâ 4:47

Mâ'ide 5:43

A'raf 7:157

"Nor did the People of the Book disagree among themselves until Clear Proof was given them."

Bakara 2:213
Al-i İmran 3:19
Shu'ara 42:14
Jathiya 45:16-17
Bayyina 98:4

"The Torah ... Whoever judges not by what Allah had revealed; such are disbelievers. We sent Jesus ... and bestowed on him the Gospel"

Al-i İmran 3:23
Mâ'ide 5:44-47
Sebe' 34:31
Mu'min 40:69-70

"Do you believe in one part of the Scripture and disbelieve in another?"

Bakara 2:61, 85
Al-i İmran 3:98
Nisâ 4:150-152
Ra'd 13:36, 43
Jumu'ah 62:5

"We sent Jesus son of Mary, confirming that which was (revealed) before him"

Al-i İmran 3:3-4, 48-50
Mâ'ide 5:46, 48
Yusuf 12:111
Ahkâf 46:12

The Bible Could Not Have Been Changed After Muhammad

The Bible could not have been changed after the time of Muhammad, because pre-Islamic Bibles say exactly the same things as those after Muhammad.

The Hebrew Dead Sea Scrolls (200 BC – AD 70)

The Dead Sea Scrolls were discovered in March of 1947 by an Arab shepherd named Muhammed el-Dib.

These manuscripts were written by the Essenes, a Jewish sect of scribes at Qumran located on the northwest side of the Dead Sea.

Over 400,000 manuscripts making up over 500 books were found dating from between 200 BC and AD 70. This is the largest find of ancient manuscripts ever discovered, and these are practically the only surviving Old Testament manuscripts written before AD 100.

These manuscripts include portions of all Old Testament books except for the book of Esther. This book was excluded by the Essenes because the name of God is not found in that book.

Although these manuscripts were written long before Muhammad, there is no significant difference between these manuscripts and the Masoretic texts of AD 1000, which were used to translate the Old Testament that we have today. The Leningrad Codex of AD 1008 agrees with the text of the Old Testament manuscripts from the Dead Sea Scrolls (1,000 years earlier) and these can be seen in Israel today where they are preserved at a museum called The Shrine of the Book.[1]

---

1   McDowell, *The New Evidence That Demands a Verdict*, pp. 77-82, 89-90.

The Greek New Testament
Manuscripts (AD 100 to AD 600)

Over 5,600 manuscripts of the Greek New Testament still exist, most of which pre-date Islam. All of these manuscripts are in agreement with each other concerning the essential doctrines of Christ.

The Greek Septuagint (c. 250 BC)[1]

The Septuagint is a translation of the Old Testament from Hebrew into Greek. It was translated during the reign of King Ptolemy II (309 BC < 274 BC) and was completed around 250 BC. Jesus and the disciples quoted from the Septuagint. It includes the *deutero-canonical* list of books, which are disputed between Catholics and Protestants (as well as the additions to Daniel and Esther). It became *the* Christian Old Testament that was in use at that time.

The Latin Vulgate (AD 384)[2]

Jerome's Latin Vulgate was a translation of the Bible from Greek manuscripts into Latin, which was used for one thousand years. Damasus I, the bishop of Rome, commissioned Jerome (also known as Hieronymus) to do this translation in AD 382, and it was completed around AD 384. There are still over eight thousand manuscripts of the Vulgate, some of which pre-date Islam, and others which were copied after Islam, but the text of all of these says the same thing.

---

1   McDowell, *Evidence that Demands a Verdict*, pp. 61-62.

2   McDowell, *The New Evidence*, pp. 20 & 34.

Qur'an Verses That Confirm Bible Legitimacy

Verses in the Qur'an affirm that Christians and Jews possessed Bibles which had not been changed at the time of Muhammad.

Bakara 2:62 – Those who believe (in the Qur'an and <u>the Prophets sent before you</u>), <u>Jews</u>, <u>Christians</u>, and Sabeans; whoever believes in Allah and the Last Day and does what is right; <u>shall be rewarded by their Lord</u>; no fear shall come upon them, neither shall they regret.

Al-i İmran 3:55 – O Jesus! I am ... setting <u>those who follow you above</u> those who disbelieve <u>until the day of Resurrection</u> ...

Al-i İmran 3:113-114 – (113) (Yet) they are not all alike. <u>Among the People of the Scripture there is an upright community who during the night recite the revelations of Allah</u> and fall prostrate before Him. (114) They believe in Allah and the Last Day, and enjoin what is right and forbid what is evil, and vie with one another in good works. <u>They are of the righteous.</u>

Al-i İmran 3:199 – And there are certainly <u>among the People of the Scripture</u> some who believe in Allah and that which is revealed to you and that which was revealed to them, humbling themselves before Allah. <u>They will not sell the revelations (signs) of Allah for a miserable gain!</u>

Nisâ 4:162 – But those of them who are firm in knowledge, and the believers, <u>believe in that</u> which is revealed to you, and that <u>which was revealed before you</u>, especially the diligent in prayer and those who pay the Zakat, the believers in Allah and the Last Day. <u>To them We shall bestow a great reward.</u>

Mâ'ide 5:66, 69 – (66) <u>If they had observed (practiced) the Torah and the Gospel and that which was revealed to them</u>

from their Lord, they would surely have been nourished from above them and from beneath their feet. Among them there are people who are moderate, but many of them are of evil conduct ... (69) Those who believe (in the Qur'an), and those who are Jews, and Sabeans, and Christians, whoso believes in Allah and the last Day and does right, no fear will come upon them, neither shall they grieve.

A'raf 7:159, 169 – (159) And of the people of Moses, there is a community who lead with truth and establish justice therewith ... (169) Has not the covenant of the scripture been taken on their behalf that they should not speak aught concerning Allah except the truth? And they have studied that which is therein. And the home of the hereafter is better, for those who fear Him. Have you no sense?

Mu'min 40:53-54 – (53) And we did give Moses the guidance and made the Children of Israel to inherit the Scripture. (54) A guide and a reminder for men of understanding.

Jathiya 45:16 – Before this, We had bestowed on the Children of Israel the Book and the Command and the Prophethood, and provided them with good things, and favored them above (all) peoples.

The Qur'an's Critique of Jews and Christians

None of the verses in the Qur'an which are "critical" of Jews and Christians indicate that they corrupted the text of the Bible.

"Why do you knowingly <u>conceal the truth</u>?"

Bakara 2:42, 159, 174

Al-i İmran 3:71

Mâ'ide 5:15

Mâ'ide 5:61

En'âm 6:91

"<u>Barter it</u> for a paltry price"

Bakara 2:41, 79, 174

Al-i İmran 3:187

Nisâ 4:44

Mâ'ide 5:44

Tevbe 9:9

"They <u>forget a part</u> of that wherewith they had been reminded"

Mâ'ide 5:13-14

"There are illiterate men among them who are <u>ignorant of the Scripture</u>"

Bakara 2:78

Al-i İmran 3:66

En'âm 6:91

"Nay, most of them <u>do not believe</u>"

Bakara 2:100
Al-i İmran 3:23
Mâ'ide 5:42-43, 62, 68

"Some factions <u>deny a part of it</u>"

Bakara 2:85
Al-i İmran 3:98
Nisâ 4:150-152
Ra'd 13:36

"You drive back believers from the Way of Allah"

Al-i İmran 3:99

"There is a party of them who distort the Scripture <u>with their tongues</u>"

Bakara 2:75 – <u>heard</u> the word of Allah and knowingly perverted it –

Al-i İmran 3:78 – who distort the Scriptures <u>with their tongues</u> ...

Nisâ 4:46 – Jews change words from their context and <u>say</u> ...

Mâ'ide 5:13, 41 – They change words ... <u>distorting with their tongues</u> ... changing words from their context and <u>saying</u> ...

En'âm 6:91 – Say (to the Jews <u>who speak thus</u>) ...

A'raf 7:162 – changed the word which had been <u>told</u> ...

What is the Purpose of God in Relation to His Holy Books?

<u>Ask the Question</u>: What is the **PURPOSE** of God in relation to His Holy Books? Does God <u>want</u> His Holy books to be changed, or corrupted? Absolutely <u>NOT</u>! Both the Bible and the Qur'an agree that God does <u>NOT</u> want His Holy Books to be corrupted or changed! Otherwise, God could not be "The Just and Righteous One" *(El-Adl)*, as He will use these Holy Books as the righteous standard by which to judge all of mankind on the day of judgment.

According to the Bible

Deuteronomy 4:2 – <u>Ye shall not add unto the word which I command you, neither shall ye diminish ought from it</u>, that ye may keep the commandments of the Lord your God which I command you.

Deuteronomy 12:32 – What thing soever I command you, observe to do it: <u>thou shalt not add thereto, nor diminish from it</u>.

Isaiah 14:24, 27 – (24) The Lord of hosts hath sworn, saying … <u>as I have purposed, *so* shall it stand</u>: (27) <u>For the Lord of hosts hath purposed, and who shall disannul *it*? and his hand *is* stretched out, and who shall turn it back?</u>

Jeremiah 36:27-28 – (27) Then the word of the Lord came to Jeremiah, after the king had burned the roll, … (28) Take thee again another roll, and <u>write in it all the former words that were in the first roll</u>.

John 12:48 – He that rejecteth me, and receiveth not <u>my words</u>, hath <u>one that judgeth</u> him: <u>the word that I have spoken, the same shall judge him in the last day</u>.

Revelation 22:19 – And <u>if any man shall take away from the words of the book of this prophecy</u>, God shall <u>take away his part out of the book of life</u>.

According to the Qur'an

A'raf 7:196 – My protecting Friend is Allah, who revealed the scripture. He befriends the righteous.

Hûd 11:57 – For my Lord is Guardian over all things.

Hijr 15:9 – We have, without doubt, sent down the Reminder, and We preserve it.

Muhammad 47:11, 32 – (11) That is because Allah is the protector of the believers and the disbelievers have no protector at all. (32) Those who disbelieve and hinder others from Allah's Way and dispute with the Messenger after the guidance has been manifested to them, can in no way harm Allah, but Allah indeed will render all their works of no effect.

Mujâdila 58:10 – Secret counsels are the work of the devil, who thereby seeks to annoy the faithful. Yet he can harm nothing at all except by Allah's leave. In Allah let the faithful put their trust.

Hashr 59:23 – He is Allah ... the Source of Security the keeper of Faith; the Guardian ...

Hakka 69:44-47 – (44) And if he had invented false sayings concerning Us, (45) We assuredly had taken him by the right hand (46) and then severed his life-artery, (47) and none of you could have held Us off from him.

Jinn 72:26-28 – (26) He (alone) knows the unseen, and does not reveal to anyone his secret. (27) Except to every messenger whom he has chosen, and then He sends down guardians who walk before him and behind him. (28) That He may know that they have indeed conveyed the message of their Lord. He surrounds all their doings, and keeps count of all things.

What is the Power of God in Relation to His Holy Books?

Ask the Question: What is the **POWER** of God in relation to His Holy Books? Is God <u>able</u> to protect His Holy Books from change and corruption? Absolutely <u>YES</u>! Both the Bible and the Qur'an agree that God is more than "able" to protect his own Holy Books! Otherwise, He would not be "God-Almighty" (*El-Kadir*).

According to the Bible

Psalm 12:6-7 – (6) <u>The words of the LORD</u> are pure words: as silver tried in a furnace of earth, purified seven times. (7) <u>Thou shalt keep them</u>. O LORD, thou shalt preserve them from this generation <u>for ever</u>.

Psalm 146:5-6 – (5) the LORD ... <u>God</u> ... (6) which <u>keepeth truth for ever</u>.

Isaiah 46:9-11 – (9) Remember the former things of old: for I am God, ... and there is none like me, (10) <u>Declaring the end from the beginning</u>, and from ancient times the things that are not yet done, saying, My counsel shall stand, and <u>I will do all my pleasure</u>: (11) ... <u>I have spoken it, I will also bring it to pass; I have purposed it, I will also do it</u>.

Isaiah 55:11 – So shall <u>my word </u>be that goeth forth out of my mouth: it <u>shall not return unto me void</u>, but it shall accomplish that which I please, and <u>it shall prosper in the thing whereto I sent it</u>.

Mark 12:24 – And Jesus answering said unto them, <u>Do ye not therefore err, because ye know not the scriptures, neither the power of God</u>?

Mark 13:31 – Heaven and earth shall pass away: but <u>my words shall not pass away</u>.

Luke 16:17 – And it is easier for heaven and earth to pass, than for <u>one tittle of the law to fail</u>.

According to the Qur'an

Bakara 2:20, 255 – (20) <u>Allah has power over all things</u> ... <u>Allah</u>! there is no god but Him, the Living, the Eternal ... (255) <u>His Throne embraces</u> the Heavens and <u>the earth</u>, and <u>it tires Him not to uphold them both</u>.

En'âm 6:114-115 – (114) Shall I seek other than <u>Allah</u> for a <u>judge</u>, when <u>He it is who has revealed to you scripture</u>, fully explained? ... (115) Perfected is the <u>Word of your Lord</u> in <u>truth and justice</u>. <u>There is nothing that can change His words</u>.

Hijr 15:9 – We have, without doubt, sent down <u>the Reminder</u>, and <u>We preserve it</u>.

Hajj 22:52 – And We never sent a messenger or prophet before you, but (without doubt) when he framed a desire, Satan cast into his desire some affair. But <u>Allah abrogates what Satan casts</u>. <u>Allah establishes (perfects) his signs (revelations)</u>.

Lokmân 31:27 – And if all the trees in the earth were pens, and the sea, with seven more seas to help it, (were ink), <u>the words of Allah could not be exhausted</u>.

Mujâdila 58:10 – <u>the devil</u> ... <u>he can harm nothing at all except by Allah's leave</u>. In Allah let the faithful put their trust.

Hakka 69:44-47 – (44) And <u>if he had invented false sayings concerning Us</u>, (45) <u>We assuredly had</u> taken him by the right hand (46) And then <u>severed his life-artery</u>, (47) and <u>none of you could have held Us off from him</u>.

Buruj 85:21-22 – (21) Indeed this is a glorious <u>Qur'an</u>, (22) <u>Preserved in a well-guarded tablet</u>.

Fundamental Errors of Logic Which Muslims Make in Relation to the Word of God

"A priori"[1]

This is an assumption relating to what can be known through an understanding of how certain things work rather than by observation; a conclusion arrived at without examination or analysis; something formed or conceived beforehand. Because the Qur'an says the Bible contains prophecies about Muhammad (A'raf 7:157 and Saf 61:6) but these are not found in the Bible, it is concluded, therefore, that the Bible must have been changed, because the Qur'an couldn't have been wrong.

"Argumentum ad ignorantium"

An attempt to gain support for some position by dwelling upon the impossibility of proving the opposite. Muslims who claim that the Bible has been changed without knowing how to read Greek or Hebrew and without any knowledge of the science of textual criticism, are guilty of speaking out of ignorance.

"Petitio principii"

Begging the question assumes the conclusion to be proved or is circular reasoning. "The Bible has been changed because it disagrees with the Qur'an."

"Argumentum ad populum"

Addresses popular feelings, passions, or prejudices, not the facts. "The Bible must be changed because most Muslims *say* that it has been changed."

"Argumentum ad verecundiam"

An appeal based upon the reverence which most people feel for a great name without considering the evidence for the arguments

---

1   The definitions on pages 48-49 for the Latin terms of logic are derived from Irving M. Copi, *Introduction to Logic*, pp. 91-107.

which are advanced for or against the position. "The Bible must have been changed because a famous German theologian once claimed that it has been changed."

"Argumentum ad hominem"

An appeal based on the character of the person against whom it is directed. "The Jews must have corrupted their Holy Books because they were such bad people."

"Ignoratio Elenchi"

An irrelevant conclusion arrived at by substituting some other proposition more or less closely related to it. "The New Testament must have been lost and corrupted because the Christians forgot some of it."

"Argumentum ad baculum"

An appeal to the big stick! Might makes right. At a mosque in an Islamic Center in New Jersey where I was the speaker in a Muslim-Christian debate on the subject of "Has the Bible Been Changed," a Muslim theologian from Turkey in the audience sided with me in defense of the Holy Books and said to the Muslim speaker, "You have lied. The Bible has not been changed!" After the Turk had said this, other Muslims at the conference surrounded him and threatened him, saying, "Don't say that again or we will kill you!"

Bakara 2:256….. There is no compulsion in religion.

"Argumentum non sequitur[1]"

The fallacy of the consequent occurs when the conclusion doesn't really follow from the premises by which it is supposed to be supported.

1. If "The Bible is the Word of God," and

2. If "No Man Can Change the Word of God,"

3. Then "The Bible Has Been Changed."

---

[1]   The Latin terms of logic on these pages are derived from Copi, Introduction to Logic, pp. 91-107.

A Correct Logical Syllogism in Relation to the Word of God

If the <u>Bible</u> Is the <u>Word of God</u>

1 Corinthians 14:37-38 – (37) <u>If any man think himself to be a prophet</u>, or spiritual, <u>let him acknowledge</u> that <u>the things that I write</u> unto you are <u>the commandments of the Lord</u>. (38) But if any man be ignorant, let him be ignorant.

Nisâ 4:136 – O you who believe! <u>Believe in</u> Allah and His messenger and the Scripture which he has revealed to His messenger <u>and the Scripture which He revealed before you.</u>

If <u>No Man Can Change the Word of God</u>

Matthew 24:35 – Heaven and earth shall pass away, <u>but my words shall not pass away.</u>

Kehf 18:27 – <u>No one can change His words.</u>

Then <u>the Bible Cannot Be Changed</u>

Isaiah 40:8 – The grass withereth, the flower fadeth: but <u>the word of our God shall stand for ever.</u>

1 Peter 1:23, 25 – (23) Being born again, not of corruptible seed, but of incorruptible, by <u>the word of God, which liveth and abideth for ever.</u> (25) But <u>the word of the Lord endureth for ever.</u>

Yunus 10:64 – <u>No change can there be in the words of Allah.</u>

Kaf 50:29 – <u>My word cannot be changed.</u>

If God Does Not Want His Holy Books to Be Changed (His Purpose)

Deuteronomy 4:2 – <u>Ye shall not add unto the word which I command you, neither shall ye diminish ought from it</u>, that ye may keep the commandments of the LORD your God which I command you.

Hijr 15:9 – We have, without doubt, sent down <u>the Reminder</u>, and <u>We preserve it</u>.

If God Is Able to Protect His Holy Books from Change (His Power)

Isaiah 55:11 – So shall <u>my word</u> be that goeth forth out of my mouth: it <u>shall not return unto me void</u>, but it shall accomplish that which I please, and <u>it shall prosper in the thing whereto I sent it</u>.

Hakka 69:44-47 – (44) And <u>if he had invented false sayings concerning Us</u>, (45) We assuredly had taken him by the right hand (46) and then severed his life-artery, (47) and <u>none of you could have held Us off from him</u>.

Then the Bible Cannot Be Changed

Matthew 5:18 – Till heaven and earth pass, <u>one jot or one tittle shall in no way pass from the law</u>, till all be fulfilled.

Mark 13:31 – Heaven and earth shall pass away: but <u>my words shall not pass away</u>.

İsra 17:77 – (Such was Our) way <u>with the messengers</u> We sent before you. And you will find <u>no change</u> in Our ways.

Did God Not Know?

Claims of corruption imply that God did not know His Holy Books would be changed.

"el-Alîm"
The Omniscient One, *#20*
who is well aware of everything.

Hebrews 4:12-13 – (12) For the <u>word of God is quick, and powerful</u>, and sharper than any twoedged sword, piercing even to the dividing asunder of soul and spirit, and of the joints and marrow, and is a discerner of the thoughts and intents of the heart. (13) <u>Neither is there any creature that is not manifest in his sight</u>: <u>but all things are naked and open unto the eyes of him</u> with whom we have to do.

Bakara 2:231 – <u>Do not make the revelations of Allah a mockery</u>. <u>Remember</u> the favors He has bestowed on you and <u>the Book</u> and the wisdom which he has revealed, wherewith He does exhort you. Fear Allah, and <u>know that He has knowledge of all things</u>.

"el-Bâsîr"
The Observant One, *#28*
who sees and hears all things.

Psalm 94:7-9 – (7) <u>Yet they say, The LORD shall not see, neither shall the God of Jacob regard it</u>. (8) Understand, <u>ye brutish</u> among the people: and <u>ye fools</u>, when will ye be wise? (9) He that planted the ear, shall he not hear? he that formed the eye, shall he not see?

Mu'min 40:56 – Assuredly, those who wrangle concerning the <u>Revelations of Allah</u> without any authority having come to them, there is nothing but pride in their hearts; but they will never attain to their ambitions. Therefore take refuge in Allah. <u>It is He Who hears and sees</u>.

"er-Rakîb"
The Watcher, #44
who keeps watch over his creation.

Isaiah 46:9-10 – (9) Remember the former things of old: for I am God, and there is none else; I am God, and there is none like me, (10) declaring the end from the beginning, and from ancient times the things that are not yet done, saying, My counsel shall stand, and I will do all my pleasure.

Mâ'ide 5:116-117 – (116) Assuredly, You only You, are the Knower of things hidden. (117) I spoke to them only that which You commanded me (saying): "Worship Allah, my Lord and your Lord." I was witness of them while I dwelt among them, and when You took me You were the Watcher over them. You are witness over all things.

"el-Hafîz"
The Guardian, #39
who keeps watch over everything.

Proverbs 2:8 – He keepeth the paths of judgment, and preserveth the way of his saints.

Hûd 11:57 – For my Lord is Guardian over all things.

Jinn 72:26-28 – (26) He (alone) knows the unseen, and does not reveal to anyone His secret. (27) Except to every messenger whom he has chosen, and then He sends down guardians who walk before him and behind him. (28) That He may know that they have indeed conveyed the message of their Lord. He surrounds all their doings, and keeps count of all things.

Did God Not Care?

Claims of corruption imply that God did not care if His Holy Books would be changed.

"el-Vedûd"
The Loving One, #48
compassionate and loving to his servants.

Jeremiah 31:3, 31, 34 – (3) The LORD hath appeared of old unto me, saying, Yea, <u>I have loved thee with an everlasting love</u>. (31) Behold, the days come, saith the LORD, that I will make <u>a new covenant</u> with the house of Israel, and with the house of Judah. (34) for I will forgive their iniquity, and <u>I will remember their sin no more</u>.

1 John 4:6, 8, 16 – (6) Hereby know we the spirit of truth, and the spirit of error. (8) He that loveth not knoweth not God; for <u>God is love</u>. (16) <u>God is love</u>; and he that dwelleth in love dwelleth in God, and God in him.

Buruj 85:14, 21-22 – (14) He is the Forgiving and <u>Loving</u> ... (21) Indeed this is a glorious <u>Qur'an</u>, (22) <u>Preserved in a well-guarded tablet</u>.

"er-Rezzâk"
The Supplier, #18
who provides for both the spiritual and
physical needs of believers.

Philippians 4:19 – But my <u>God shall supply all your need</u> according to his riches in glory by Christ Jesus.

Tur 51:58 – <u>Allah</u>! He it is that <u>gives livelihood</u>, the Lord of unbreakable might.

"er-Reshîd"
The Guide, #98
who leads believers towards perfection.

Psalm 48:14 – For this God is our God <u>for ever</u> and ever: <u>he will be our guide even unto death</u>.

Psalm 119:9, 105 – (9) Wherewithal shall a young man cleanse his way? by taking heed thereto according to <u>thy word</u>. (105) <u>Thy word</u> is a <u>lamp unto my feet</u>, and <u>a light unto my path</u>.

Kehf 18:17, 23-24 – (17) He whom <u>Allah guides</u> is rightly guided … (23) Do not say of anything: "I will do it tomorrow," (24) Without adding, "If God wills." When you forget, remember your Lord, and say, "<u>May Allah guide me</u> and bring me nearer to Truth."

"el-Kuddûs"
The Most Holy One, #5
to whom all in heaven and on earth ascribe holiness.

Isaiah 40:25-26 – (25) To whom then will ye liken me, or shall I be equal? saith <u>the Holy One</u>. (26) Lift up your eyes on high, and behold <u>who hath created these *things*</u>, that bringeth out their host by number: he calleth them all by names by the greatness of his might, for that <u>*he is* strong in power</u>; <u>not one faileth</u>.

Jumu'ah 62:1 – <u>Whatever is in the heavens and in the earth</u> glorifies Allah, the Sovereign Lord, <u>the Holy One</u>, the Mighty, the Wise.

Could God Not Stop the Changes?

Claims of corruption imply that God could not do anything about His Holy Books being changed.

"el-Kadir"
The All-Powerful One, #69
who is able to do what he pleases.

Job 33:12 – Behold, <u>in this thou are not just</u>: I will answer thee, that <u>God is greater than man</u>.

Isaiah 14:24, 27 – (24) The LORD of hosts hath sworn, saying, <u>Surely as I have thought, so shall it come to pass</u>; and <u>as I have purposed, so shall it stand</u>. (27) For <u>the LORD of hosts hath purposed, and who shall disannul it</u>?

Bakara 2:20, 255 – (20) Allah has <u>power over all things</u> ... (255) Allah! there is no god but Him, the Living, the Eternal. Neither slumber nor sleep overtakes Him ... His Throne embraces the Heavens and the earth, and <u>it tires Him not to uphold them both</u>.

"el-Kebir"
The Great One, #38
who is both high and eminent.

Isaiah 57:15 – For thus saith <u>the high and lofty One</u> that inhabiteth eternity, whose name *is* Holy; <u>I dwell in the high and holy place</u>, with him also *that is* of a contrite and humble spirit, to revive the spirit of the humble, and to revive the heart of the contrite ones.

Hajj 22:62 – That is because <u>Allah, He is the Truth</u>, and that which they call instead of Him, is the False; and because <u>Allah, He is the High, the Great</u>.

"el-Jebbar"
The All-Powerful One, #10
whose might and power is absolute.

Psalm 24:8, 10 – (8) Who is this King of glory? The LORD strong and mighty, the LORD mighty in battle. (10) Who is this King of glory? The LORD of hosts, he is the King of glory. Selah.

Hashr 59:23 – He is Allah besides whom there is no other god. He is Sovereign Lord, the Holy One, the Source of security, the Keeper of Faith, the Guardian, the Mighty One, the All-Powerful, the Proud!

Hakka 69:44-47 – (44) And if he had invented false sayings concerning Us, (45) We assuredly had taken him by the right hand (46) And then severed his life-artery, (47) And none of you could have held Us off from him.

"el-Muktedir"
The Prevailer, #70
who prevails, having evil men in his powerful grip.

1 Samuel 2:9-10 – (9) He will keep the feet of his saints, and the wicked shall be silent in darkness; for by strength shall no man prevail. (10) The adversaries of the LORD shall be broken to pieces; out of heaven shall he thunder upon them: the LORD shall judge the ends of the earth.

Kehf 18:45 – Allah has power over all things.

Kamer 54:42 – But they disbelieve all Our signs and We smote them with the grasp of one Mighty, and Powerful.

Is God Not Faithful?

Claims of corruption imply that God was not faithful enough to protect His Holy Books from being changed.

"el-Mü'min"
The Faithful One, #7
who can be trusted.

Psalm 119:89-90 – (89) <u>For ever</u>, O LORD, <u>thy word is settled</u> in heaven. (90) Thy faithfulness is <u>unto all generations</u>.

Titus 1:2 – In hope of eternal life, which <u>God, that cannot lie</u>, promised before the world began.

Tevbe 9:111 – That is <u>a promise binding</u> upon Allah in the Torah and the Gospel and the Qur'an. <u>Who is more faithful to his promise than Allah?</u>

Hashr 59:23 – He is <u>Allah</u> besides whom there is no other god. He is the Sovereign Lord, the Holy One, the Source of Security, <u>the keeper of Faith</u>; the Guardian, the Mighty One, the All Powerful.

Al-i İmran 3:9, 94 – (9) <u>Allah doesn't fail the promise</u> ... (94) You never break <u>the promise</u>!

"el-Velî"
The Guardian, #78
who protects his saints as a close friend.

Nehemiah 9:6 – Thou, even <u>thou, art LORD</u> alone; thou hast made heaven, the heaven of heavens, with all their host, the earth, and all things that are therein, the seas, and all that is therein, and <u>thou preservest them all</u>.

A'raf 7:196 – My <u>protecting Friend is Allah</u>, who revealed <u>the scripture</u>. He befriends the righteous.

"el-Hâdî"
The Guide, #94
who leads and guides in safe paths.

Psalm 25:9 – <u>The meek will he guide in judgment</u>; and the meek will he teach his way.

Psalm 73:24 – Thou shalt <u>guide me</u> with <u>thy counsel</u>, and afterward receive me to glory.

Hajj 22:54 – And surely <u>Allah guides</u> those who believe <u>to the straight path</u>.

"el-Müheymin"
The Preserver, #8
who watches over and protects his people.

Psalm 12:6-7 – (6) The <u>words of the Lord</u> are pure words: as silver tried in a furnace of earth, purified seven times. (7) Thou shalt keep them, O Lord, <u>thou shalt preserve them from this generation for ever</u>.

Psalm 121:7-8 – (7) The Lord shall <u>preserve thee</u> from all evil: he shall <u>preserve thy soul</u>. (8) The Lord shall <u>preserve thy going out</u> and thy <u>coming in</u> from this time forth, and even <u>for evermore</u>.

Psalm 25:14 – The secret of the Lord *is* with them that fear him; and <u>he will shew them his covenant</u>.

Hashr 59:23 – He is <u>Allah</u> besides whom there is no other god. He is the Sovereign Lord, the Holy One, <u>the Source of Security</u>, the keeper of Faith; the <u>Guardian</u>, the Mighty One, the All Powerful ...

Is God Not Righteous?

Claims of corruption imply that God was not righteous enough to protect the holy standard by which He will judge all mankind on the day of judgment.

"el-Adl"
The Just and Righteous One, *#30*
whose word is perfect in veracity and justice.

2 Timothy 3:16 – <u>All scripture is</u> given by inspiration of God, and is profitable for doctrine, for reproof, for correction, <u>for instruction in righteousness</u>: that the man of God may be perfect.

En'âm 6:115 – Perfected is the <u>Word of your Lord</u> in <u>truth and justice</u>. <u>There is nothing that can change His words</u>. He is the Hearer and Knower.

"el-Hakem"
The Judge, *#29*
who settles all disputes.

Psalm 96:13 – Rejoice before the LORD: for he cometh, for <u>he cometh to judge the earth</u>: he <u>shall judge the world</u> with righteousness, and the people <u>with his truth</u>.

John 12:48 – He that rejecteth me, and receiveth not my words, hath one that judgeth him: <u>the word that I have spoken, the same shall judge him in the last day</u>.

Mâ'ide 5:47 – <u>Let the people of the Gospel judge by that which Allah had revealed therein</u>.

En'âm 6:114 – Shall I seek other than <u>Allah</u> for a <u>judge</u>, when <u>He it is who has revealed to you scripture</u>, fully explained?

"el-Hakk"
The Truth, #52
who is genuine and true.

Psalm 119:142, 144 – (142) Thy righteousness is an everlasting righteousness, and thy law is truth. (144) The righteousness of thy testimonies is everlasting: give me understanding, and I shall live.

2 Timothy 2:15 – Study to shew thyself approved unto God, a workman that needeth not to be ashamed, rightly dividing the word of truth.

Al-i İmran 3:55 – Allah said to Jesus! I am ... setting those who follow you above those who disbelieve until the day of Resurrection.

Hakka 69:2, 51 – (2) What is the Reality? (51) It is absolute truth.

"el-Nûr"
The Light, #93
who illuminates both heaven and earth.

Psalm 119:105 – Thy word is a lamp unto my feet, and a light unto my path.

Nur 24:35 – Allah is the Light of the heavens and of earth ... It is light upon Light. Allah guides whom He wills to His Light; and Allah sets forth parables to men, for Allah is knower of all things.

Is God Not Merciful?

Claims of corruption imply that God was not merciful enough to preserve His Holy Books for the salvation of all mankind.

"er-Rahîm"
The Compassionate, #3
who is gentle and full of compassion.

Psalm 103:8, 17-18 – (8) The LORD is merciful and gracious, slow to anger, and plenteous in mercy. (17) But the mercy of the LORD is from everlasting to everlasting upon those that fear him, and his righteousness unto children's children; (18) to such as keep his covenant, and to those that remember his commandments to do them.

Bakara 2:143 – He is Kind and Merciful to mankind.

İsra 17:66 – your Lord is ever Merciful towards you.

"el-Mukît"
The Provider, #40
who abundantly gives physical and
spiritual food to all his creation.

Genesis 22:14 – And Abraham called the name of that place Jehovah-jireh [The LORD will provide] as it is said to this day.

Psalm 145:8-9 – (8) The LORD is gracious, and full of compassion; slow to anger, and of great mercy. (9) The LORD is good to all: and his tender mercies are over all his works.

Nisâ 4:85 – Allah oversees all things.

"er-Rahmân"
The Merciful, #2
the most merciful of those who show mercy.

Isaiah 54:10 – But <u>my kindness shall not depart from thee, neither shall the covenant of my peace be removed,</u> saith the LORD that hath <u>mercy</u> on thee.

Deuteronomy 7:9 – Know therefore that the LORD thy God, he is <u>God, the faithful God, which keepeth covenant and mercy with them who love him and keep his commandments to a thousand generations</u>.

Fatih 1:1-2, 5 – (1) Praise be to Allah, the Lord of the Worlds; (2) the <u>Compassionate, the Merciful</u> ... (5) Guide us to the <u>Straight Way</u>.

"el-Vehhâb"
The Liberal Giver, #17
who gives freely of his bounty.

Psalm 119:130, 160 – (130) The <u>entrance of thy words</u> giveth light. (160) Thy word is true from the beginning: and every one of thy righteous judgments <u>endureth for ever</u>.

Al-i İmran 3:7-9 – (7) It is <u>He Who has revealed to you the Qur'an</u> ... (8) Our Lord ... bestow upon us mercy from your Presence. Assuredly, you are <u>the Bestower</u> ... (9) <u>Allah does not fail the promise</u>.

Sad 38:9, 35 – (9) your Lord, the Mighty, <u>the Bestower</u> ... (35) Surely <u>you are the Bestower</u>.

Did Satan Win the Battle for the Bible?

Claims of corruption belittle God and exalt Satan by implying that Satan won the battle for the Bible over God-Almighty.

"el-Azim"
The Great and Mighty One, *#20*
he who is above all is high and mighty.

1 Chronicles 29:11 – Thine, O LORD, *is* the greatness, and the power, and the glory, and the victory, and the majesty: for all *that is* in the heaven and in the earth *is thine*; thine *is* the kingdom, O LORD, and thou art exalted as head above all.

Bakara 2:255 – Allah! there is no god but Him, the Living, the Eternal. His Throne embraces the Heavens and the earth, and it tires Him not to uphold them both.

"el-Kahhar"
The Dominator, *#16*
who powerfully avenges and overcomes all.

Deuteronomy 32:39 – See now that I, *even* I, *am* he, and *there is* no god with me: I kill, and I make alive; I wound, and I heal: neither *is there any* that can deliver out of my hand.

Psalm 33:9-11 – (9) For he spake, and it was done; he commanded, and it stood fast. (10) The LORD bringeth the counsel of the heathen to nought: he maketh the devices of the people of none effect. (11) The counsel of the LORD standeth for ever, the thoughts of his heart to all generations.

Hajj 22:52 – And We never sent a messenger or prophet before you, but (without doubt) when he framed a desire, Satan cast into his desire some affair. But Allah abrogates what Satan casts. Allah establishes (perfects) his signs (revelations), and Allah is All-Knowing, All-Wise.

"el-Azîz"
The Mighty One, #94
who is mighty in his sublime sovereignty.

Isaiah 1:24 – Therefore saith the Lord, the LORD of hosts, <u>the mighty One of İsrael</u>, Ah, <u>I will ease me of mine adversaries</u>, and avenge me of mine enemies.

Hashr 59:23 – <u>He is Allah</u> besides whom there is no other god. He is Sovereign Lord, the Holy One, the Source of security, the Keeper of Faith, the Guardian, <u>the Mighty One</u>, <u>the All-Powerful</u> ...

Muhammad 47:32 – <u>Those who disbelieve</u> and hinder others from Allah's Way and dispute with the Messenger after the guidance has been manifested to them, <u>can in no way harm Allah, but Allah indeed will render all their works of no effect</u>.

"el-Kavi"
The Strong and Powerful One, #54
who is sublime in his strength and his power.

2 Chronicles 16:9 – For the eyes of the LORD run to and fro throughout the whole earth, <u>to shew himself strong in the behalf of them whose heart is perfect toward him</u>.

Hajj 22:74 – They do not esteem Allah His rightful measure. Truly <u>Allah is Strong, Almighty</u>.

Enfal 8:52 – Assuredly <u>Allah is Strong</u>, Severe in punishment.

The Hypocritical Nature of the Claim That the Bible Has Been Changed

Muslims who say, "The Bible has been changed" should consider whether or not they are implying that either 1) <u>God did not know</u>, or that 2) <u>He did not care</u>, or that 3) <u>He couldn't do anything about it</u>. When you think about what is implied in this statement, there are no other options available. At least one or all three of these fallacies can be implied! Any one of these could be considered a blasphemy against the character attributes of God as found in both the Bible and the Qur'an in the ninety-nine names of God (the *Esmaül-Hüsna*) as previously listed (see pp. 50-62). According to the Qur'an, ignorant people (*jahiliyah*) who are unwittingly blaspheming these names and character attributes of God put themselves under the curse of being "hypocrites" (*zindiq*) and "unbelievers" (*kafir*) who are condemned to hell (see pp. 33-34).

If a Muslim says, "The Bible has been changed," are they not in fact implying that God is guilty of having a hypocritical double standard in protecting one of the Holy Books (that is, the Qur'an) while not protecting all of the other Holy Books (the *Tevrat, Zebur, and İnjil*)? God does not have a double standard, and on this subject, the Qur'an correctly teaches that the *Tevrat, Zebur*, and İnjil are the Word of God and that no man can ever change the Word of God! If God protects one of the Holy Books, He will obviously protect all of them in exactly the same way, because this is His eternal standard by which He will judge all mankind on the day of judgment (cf. John 12:48 and Revelation 20:12).

If a Muslim says, "I believe in all of the Holy Books which God has sent," but at the same time willfully refuses to read the Bible because he says, "The Bible has been changed," this person is in reality guilty of implying that God has a double standard in relation to His Holy Books. *Haşa!* (God forbid!) "<u>Repent</u>, for the kingdom of heaven is at hand." (Matthew 3:2)

Muslims Are Not Allowed to Make Any Distinction Between the Holy Books

Bakara 2:136, 285 – (136) Say (O Muslims): <u>We believe in</u> Allah and <u>that which is revealed to</u> us, and that which is revealed to Abraham, Ishmael, Isaac, Jacob, and the tribes; to <u>Moses and Jesus and the (other) prophets by their Lord.</u> (285) <u>"We make no distinction between any of His messengers"</u> – and they say: "We hear and obey."

If the Qur'an Is Protected by God, Then According to the Qur'an, the Bible Must Also Be Protected by God

Buruj 85:21-22 – (21) Indeed this is a glorious <u>Qur'an,</u> (22) <u>Preserved in a well-guarded tablet.</u>

Tevbe 9:111 – That is a <u>promise binding upon Allah</u> in the <u>Torah</u> and the <u>Gospel</u> and the <u>Qur'an.</u>

Hijr 15:9 – We have, without doubt, sent down <u>the Reminder,</u> and <u>we preserve it.</u>

Are Not Lies about the Bible Being Corrupted Truly Evil in the Sight of God?

En'âm 6:93 – <u>Who is guilty of more wrong than he who forges a lie against Allah,</u> or says: "I am inspired," when he is not inspired in anything.

Yunus 10:17 – <u>Who is more wicked than the man</u> who invents a lie about Allah and <u>denies His revelations?</u> Truly the evil-doers shall not succeed.

The Detailed Care Taken in Copying the Old Testament

The Talmudists (AD 100-500)

The Talmudists had quite an intricate system for transcribing synagogue scrolls. **Davidson** states: "These copyists (*grammateis*) were at first called *Sopherim* (from the Hebrew word meaning "to count"), because, as the Talmud says, 'they counted all the letters in the Torah.' For example, there are 5,845 sentences in the Torah. The middle letter in the Torah is in Leviticus 11:42, the letter *vav* in the word *gâchôn,* meaning 'belly.' The middle word in the Torah is in Leviticus 10:16, *dârash*, meaning 'friend.' The middle verse in the Torah is Leviticus 13:33."[1]

Ramm points out that they would count the number of letters on each new page vertically, horizontally, and diagonally, and they would count each syllable and paragraph for uniformity. If there were any discrepancies from the original, they would either burn or bury that copy and start all over.[2]

Jeffrey gives the following statistics on the exact number of Hebrew letters used in the Torah:[3]

Alef	42,377	*Teyth*	11,052	*Peh*	22,725
Beth	38,218	*Yod*	66,420	*Tsadey*	21,882
Giymel	29,537	*Kaph*	48,253	*Kohf*	22,972
Dalet	32,530	*Lamed*	41,517	*Reys*	22,147
He'	47,754	*Mem*	77,778	*Şin*	32,148
Vav	76,922	*Nun*	41,696	*Tav*	59,343
Zahyin	22,867	*Şamek*	13,580		
Keth	23,447	*'Ayin*	20,175		

1   Samuel Davidson, *The Hebrew Text of the Old Testament*, p. 89.
2   Bernard Ramm, *Protestant Christian Evidences*, pp. 230-231.
3   Grant Jeffrey, *The Signature of God*, p. 14.

Regulations of the Talmudists[1]

1. A synagogue roll must be written on the skins of clean animals.

2. Prepared for the particular use of the synagogue by a Jew.

3. These must be fastened together with strings taken from clean animals.

4. Every skin must contain a certain number of columns, equal throughout the entire codex.

5. The length of each column must not extend over less than 48 or more than 60 lines; and the breadth must consist of 30 letters.

6. The whole copy must be first-lined; and if three words be written without a line, it is worthless.

7. The ink should be black ... and be prepared according to a definite recipe.

8. An authentic copy must be the examplar, from which the transcriber ought not in the least deviate.

9. No word or letter, not even a *yod*, must be written from memory, the scribe not having looked at the codex before him.

10. Between every consonant the space of a hair or thread must intervene,

11. Between every new *parashah*, or section, the breadth of nine consonants,

12. Between every book, three lines.

13. The fifth Book of Moses must terminate exactly with a line; but the rest need not do so.

14. The copyist must sit in full Jewish dress,

15. wash his whole body,

16. not begin to write the name of God with a pen newly dipped in ink,

17. and should a king address him while writing that name he must take no notice of him.

---

1   Davidson, *The Hebrew Text of the Old Testament*, p. 89.

Textual Manuscript Evidence for the Holy Books

For The Bible

At present, no one has found original copies of either the Bible or the Qur'an. However, there are over 5,600 ancient Greek manuscripts of the New Testament still in existence today which pre-date Islam, and all of these manuscripts teach the same fundamental doctrines of Christ, which were accepted by the early church fathers from the time of Christ to this present day. There are no textual manuscript differences that affect any of the fundamental doctrines which Christians have always believed.[1]

For The Qur'an

While Christian theological schools do offer courses on the science of textual criticism for the Bible to compare the most ancient copies of the earliest manuscripts, in Islamic theological schools there are no courses offered in the science of textual criticism for the origins of the Qur'an. Muslims are not allowed to question the validity of any aspect of the Qur'an or Muhammad (Mâ'ide 5:101). Because there are many conflicts between the Bible and the Qur'an, and based upon an *a priori* assumption that the Qur'an could not possibly be wrong, Muslims are therefore forced to claim that the Bible has been changed. Because the third Caliph, Uthman (AD 644–656), collected and burned all the variant copies of the Qur'an twenty years after Muhammad's death, Muslims assume that Christians have done something similar with the original text of the Bible. This is a simple example of the fallacy of an *ignoratio elenchi.* (see p.43).

Zumer 39:9 – <u>Can those who know and those who do not know ever be equal</u>? But only men of understanding will pay heed.

---

1 McDowell, *Evidence That Demands a Verdict*, pp. 46-50.

For The New Testament

The Muratorian Canon: Written in Greek and dated from around AD 180, it is one of the oldest known lists of the books of the New Testament. It was discovered in 1740 in Milan in the Ambrosian Library by a librarian named Muratori.

Below are a list of just a few of the ancient manuscripts from the Greek New Testament which are still in existence today all of which predate Islam.[1]

Bodmer Papyrus: (p66, p72, p75) AD 125–225
Codex Ephraemi Rescriptus: (Codex C) AD 400–450
Codex Florentinus: (Codex 0171) AD 400
Codex Berolinensis: (Codex 0188) 4th Century AD
Codex Koridethi: (Codex Koridethi) 4th Century AD
Codex Beazae Canabrigiensis: (Codex D-05) AD 450
Codex Claromontanus: (Codex D-06, D-02) AD 400–500
Codex Washingtonesis: (Codex W-032) AD 450–550
Oxyrhyncus Papyrus: (p51, p70, p71) AD 200–300
Codex Alexandrinus: (Codex A) AD 325
Codex Vatikanus: (Codex B) AD 325–350
Codex Sinaticus: (Codex Aleph) AD 340–350
John Rylands Papyrus: (p52) AD 117–138
Arsinoe Papyrus: (p2 1388) AD 125
Chester Beatty Papyrus: (p45, p46, p47) AD 200–250

Below are listed the different types of ancient Greek New Testament manuscripts which are still in existence today.[2]

Uncials	307	(written in a formal style)
Miniscules	2,860	(smaller connected letters)
Lectionaries	2,410	(verses used for liturgy)
Papyri	109	(portions written on paper)
Total:	**5,686**	

---

1   McDowell, *Evidence That Demands a Verdict*, pp. 48-50.
2   McDowell, *The New Evidence That Demands a Verdict*, pp. 38-41.

Bible Textual Agreement and Uniformity

Early translations of the Bible which pre-date Islam show textual agreement and uniformity:

The Septuagint: (c. AD 250) One of the oldest translations of the Old Testament which was translated into the Greek directly from the Hebrew. In the first century AD, Greek was the *lengua-franca* of the world, and both Christ and His disciples used this translation of the Old Testament. The fact that the New Testament writers frequently quoted from the Septuagint shows how much this translation was trusted.

The Samaritan Pentateuch: (AD 100–200) This translation of the Old Testament was used for the Samaritans and it can still be seen in Samaria.

Aquila's Translation: (AD 130–160) This is another translation of the Old Testament into Greek done by Aquila.

Jerome's Latin Vulgate: (AD 384) This translation of the Old Testament into Latin was done directly from the Hebrew. Ten thousand-plus copies are still extant.

Syriac Translations: The Peshitta was done between the second and third centuries AD and is a Syriac version of the Old Testament. The Philoxenian Syriac Version was made by a translator named Polycarp about AD 508. It was revised by Heraclea in AD 616.

Aethopic Old Testament: When the disciples of Muhammad fled from Mecca before the *Hijrah*, and took refuge in Abyssinia, they found the Christians there reading the Aethopic Old Testament as well as the New Testament. This version was so old as to be difficult for the Abyssinians themselves to understand, for it had been made about the fourth century AD from the Septuagint.

Coptic Translations: When Umar conquered Egypt, he found that most of the people were Christians. They had translated the Old Testament from the Septuagint into at least three Coptic dialects: Buhairic, Sa'idic, and Bushmuric, around the third or fourth century or earlier.[1]

---

1   McDowell, *The New Evidence That Demands a Verdict*, pp. 41-42.

Pre-Islamic Translations of the Old Testament[1]

Septuagint	AD 285–247)
The Samaritan Pentateuch	AD 100–200)
Greek	Aquila (AD 130)
Syriac Peshitta	Melito (2nd century AD)
Coptic	(2nd–3rd century AD)
Aramaic	Johnathan ben Uzeyl (AD 320)
Aethopic	(4th century AD)
Latin Vulgate	Jerome (AD 405)
Armenian	(AD 411)
Gothic	Ulphilas (AD 360)
Philoxenian Syriac	Polycarp (AD 508)

Number of Extant Copies of Pre-Islamic Translations of the New Testament[2]

Latin Vulgate	10,000 +
Aethopic	2,000 +
Slavic	4,101
Armenian	2,587
Syriac Peshitta	350 +
Buhairic	100
Arabic	75
Old Latin	50
Anglo Saxon	7
Gothic	6
Sogdian	3
Old Syriac	2
Persian	2
Frankish	1

Total: 19,284

---

1   McDowell, *Evidence That Demands a Verdict*, pp. 52-53.
2   McDowell, *The New Evidence That Demands a Verdict*, pp. 34, 41.

The Degree of Textual Agreement and Uniformity in the Ancient Manuscripts

The Degree of Uniformity in the Manuscripts of the Old Testament

If all the extant Old Testament manuscripts are compared, they show that only one letter out of every 1,580 letters are different at all. This shows only a 0.06 percent difference among the manuscripts, or that they are 99.94 percent the same.[1]

The Degree of Uniformity in the Manuscripts of the New Testament

For the New Testament, out of the 5,600 ancient manuscripts which we have, in approximately 20,000 lines of the New Testament, only 40 lines – found mostly in 19 passages – or about 400 words show any difference at all. Out of the 7,957 verses in the New Testament, there are only 19 doubtful passages containing 41 verses. This shows that there is only about a 1.77 percent difference among the ancient manuscripts. In other words, we are 98.33 percent certain of the original wording in the New Testament manuscripts. Of the 400 different words, only about 40-50 make any difference in the meaning of the text, and none of these affect any Christian doctrine or belief in the least. On the next page is a complete list of the 19 places in the New Testament where there is some doubt as to the original reading. Most study Bibles have footnotes on these verses indicating that there is some question about the correct reading of these verses in the original manuscripts. However, none of these questionable passages have any bearing on the fundamental doctrines which Christians have always believed.[2]

---

1   McDowell, *The Best of Josh McDowell: A Ready Defense*, pp. 43-46.
2   Geisler & Nix, *A General Introduction to the Bible*, pp. 361-367.

The 19 Questionable Passages
in the New Testament[1]

Matthew 17:21 – this kind goest not out but by prayer and fasting.

Mathew 18:11 – the Son of man is come to save that which was lost.

Matthew 24:14 – And this gospel ... and then shall the end come.

Mark 7:16 – If any man have ears to hear, let him hear.

Mark 9:48 – their worm dieth not, and the fire is not quenched.

Mark 11:26 – But if ye do not forgive, neither will your Father which is in heaven forgive your trespasses.

Mark 15:28 – he was numbered with the transgressors.

Mark 16:9-20 – (Has been called a later addition to the book of Mark.).

Luke 17:36 – the one shall be taken, and the other left.

Luke 23:17 – For of necessity he must release one unto them.

John 5:4 – whosoever then first after the troubling of the water stepped in was made whole.

John 7:53-8:11 – (Has been called a later addition to the original text.)

John 9:35 – Doest thou believe on the Son of God?

Acts 8:37 – If thou believest with all thine heart, thou mayest.

Acts 15:35 – Paul also and Barnabas continued in Antioch.

Acts 24:8 – Commanding his accusers to come.

Acts 28:29 – the Jews departed, and had great reasoning among themselves.

Romans 16:24 – The grace of our Lord Jesus Christ be with you all.

1 John 5:7 – For there are three that bear record.

---

1   **Note:** These verses are duly noted in most study Bibles.

The Patristics

(Early Church Fathers)

Seven of the most prolific writers during the first several centuries of Christianity were[1]:

Clement (30-100): Bishop of Rome, holding office from AD 92 until his death in AD 99. He is considered to be the first apostolic father of the church.

Justin (100-165): was an early Christian apologist, and is regarded as the foremost interpreter of the theory of the *Logos* in the second century. He was martyred alongside some of his students.

Irenaeus (130-202): Bishop of Lugdunum in Gaul, then a part of the Roman Empire. He was an early church father and apologist, and his writings were formative in the early development of Christian theology.

Tertullian (160-240): a prolific early Christian author from Carthage in the Roman province of Africa. He is the first Christian author to produce an extensive corpus of Latin Christian literature.

Hippolytus (170-235): the most important third-century theologian in the Christian church in Rome, where he was probably born.

Origen (185-254): also known as Origen Adamantius, was a scholar and early Christian theologian who was born and spent the first half of his career in Alexandria.

Eusebius (260-340): was a Roman historian of Greek descent, an exegete, and a Christian polemicist. He became the bishop of Caesarea about AD 314.

Other important early church fathers were:

Papias	(35-107)	**Athanasius**	(293-373)
Ignatius	(35-117)	**Gregory**	(329-388)
Polycarp	(70-156)	**Basil**	(330-379)
Tatian	(110-165)	**Jerome**	(342-420)
Clement	(150-215)	**Chrysostom**	(345-405)
Cyprian	(200-258)	**Augustine**	(354-430)

---

1   McDowell, *The New Evidence That Demands a Verdict*, pp. 43-45, 54.

The early church fathers quoted many verses from the New Testament in the various books which they wrote. Their quotations of the many Bible verses which they used in their writings match exactly the Greek text which is found in the earliest copies of the Greek New Testament, which can be seen in over 5,600 early manuscripts that still exist today. The quotations found in these ancient books confirm the accuracy and truthfulness of the existing ancient Greek manuscripts. All but eleven verses of the New Testament can be found quoted in the writings of the Patristics.[1]

Writer	Gospels	Acts	Paul's Epistles	Other Letters	Reve-lation	Totals
Clement AD 30–100	1,017	44	1,127	207	11	2,406
Justin AD 89–163	268	10	43	6	3	330
Iranaeus AD 130–202	1,038	194	499	23	65	1,819
Tertullian AD 160–240	3,822	502	2,609	120	205	7,258
Hippolytus AD 170–235	734	42	387	27	188	1,378
Origen AD 185–254	9,231	349	7,778	399	165	17,922
Eusebius AD 260–340	3,258	211	1,592	88	27	5,176
(Totals)	19,368	1,352	14,035	870	664	**36,289**

---

1   McDowell, *The New Evidence That Demands a Verdict*, pp. 43.

The Cardinal Doctrines of Christ

The original Greek manuscripts, the translations of the New Testament into other languages, the writings of the early church fathers, and the decisions which were made at the early church councils about the canonical books, all confirm the deity of Christ and the other fundamental doctrines of the faith which all Christians believe today. The original Greek New Testament agrees 100 percent with the message of the writings of the early church fathers and with the message found in the other New Testament translations. The text of the New Testament and more than 36,000 verses quoted in the writings of the Patristics show clearly that these early church fathers were in <u>100 percent agreement</u> about the following cardinal doctrines of Christ which are found in the Bible:

The Virgin Birth of Christ .... Matthew 1:18-21

The Sinlessness of Christ .... Hebrews 4:14-15

The Deity of Christ ....John 20:28-29

The Incarnation of Christ .... Philippians 2:5-11

The Eternality of Christ ....Hebrews 13:8

The Atoning Death of Christ .... Isaiah 53:5-12

The Omniscience of Christ .... John 4:25-26

The Omnipotence of Christ .... John 20:30-31

The Creative Power of Christ ....Colossians 1:15-22

Christ is the Word of God ....John 1:1-14

Christ is the Son of God .... Mark 14:61-62

Christ is the Messiah .... Matthew 16:16-20

Christ is the Savior of the World .... 1 John 4:14-15

Christ is the Mediator between God and Man..1 Timothy 2:5

Christ Alone Can Forgive Sin .... Mark 2:5-11

The Qur'an Affirms the Following Biblical Doctrines Concerning Christ[1]

Jesus Christ is the Son of Mary	Bakara 2:87
Jesus Christ is the Messiah	Ali-İmran 3:45
Jesus Christ is the Servant of Allah	Nisâ 4:172
Jesus Christ is a prophet	Meryem 19:30
Jesus Christ is an apostle of Allah	Mâ'ide 5:75
Jesus Christ is the Word of Allah	Al-i-İmran 3:3
Jesus Christ is the Word of Truth	Meryem 19:34
Jesus Christ is the Spirit of Allah	Tahrîm 66:12
Jesus Christ is a sign for mankind	Meryem 19:21
Jesus Christ is a witness	Nisâ 4:159
Jesus Christ is a mercy from Allah	Meryem 19:21
Jesus Christ is great (eminent)	Al-i-İmran 3:45
Jesus Christ is righteous	Al-i-İmran 3:46
Jesus Christ is blessed	Meryem 19:31
Jesus Christ did miracles	Bakara 2:87
Jesus Christ was led by the Holy Spirit	Bakara 2:253
Jesus Christ was born of a virgin	Al-i-İmran 3:47
Jesus Christ guides to the truth	Al-i-İmran 3:49
Jesus Christ healed people	Al-i-İmran 3:49
Jesus Christ raised the dead	Al-i-İmran 3:49
Jesus Christ would die for unbelievers	Al-i-İmran 3:55
Jesus Christ was resurrected from the dead	Al-i-İmran 3:55
Jesus Christ ascended to heaven	Al-i-İmran 3:55
Jesus Christ is a life giver	Mâ'ide 5:110
Jesus Christ is holy	Meryem 19:19
Jesus Christ is coming again	Zuhruf 43:61
Jesus Christ knows the future	Zuhruf 43:61, 63
Jesus Christ is to be obeyed and followed	Zuhruf 43:63

1 Timothy 4:15-16 – (15) Meditate upon these things; give thyself wholly to them; that thy profiting may appear to all. (16) Take heed unto thyself, and unto the doctrine; continue in them: for in doing this thou shalt both save thyself, and them that hear thee.

---

1   Adan İbn İsma'il, *The Belief of Isma'il*, pp. 37-38.

What Happened at the Early Church Councils?

Council of Nicea
May 20–June 19, 325 AD

Emperor Constantine invited bishops and church fathers, and approximately 318 bishops attended this first church council. Only three people in attendance recorded the proceedings of this council: Eusebius of Caesarea, Athanasius of Alexandria, and Eustathius of Antioch. The purpose of the council was to debate whether or not Christ was divine. The subject of which books were considered to be canonical was not discussed at this council. However, the collective decisions which were made are reflected in the **Nicene Creed**[1] given below.

We believe in one God, the Father Almighty, Maker of all things visible and invisible. And in one Lord Jesus Christ, the Son of God, begotten of the Father [the only-begotten; that is, of the essence of the Father, God of God], Light of Light, very God of very God, begotten, not made, being of one substance with the Father; By whom all things were made [both in heaven and on earth]; Who for us men, and for our salvation, came down and was incarnate and was made man; He suffered, and the third day he rose again, ascended into heaven; From thence he shall come to judge the quick and the dead. And in the Holy Ghost. [But those who say: 'There was a time when he was not'; and 'He was not before he was made'; and 'He was made out of nothing,' or 'He is of another substance' or 'essence,' or 'The Son of God is created,' or 'changeable,' or 'alterable' – they are condemned by the holy catholic and apostolic Church.]

These church councils finally resolved all question as to what

1   *Wikipedia*: Council of Nicea and Nicene Creed

constituted the canon of the New Testament. In his Easter letter of 367, Athanasius, bishop of Alexandria, gave a list of exactly the same twenty-seven books that would formally become the New Testament canon.[1]

Council of Laodicea
AD 336

Recognized and accepted all books of the New Testament canon except Revelation. But at the following three councils it was also accepted.

Council of Hippo
AD 393

The list of twenty-seven books which are currently in the New Testament was officially accepted by the Orthodox church.

Councils of Carthage
AD 397 and AD 419

These councils took place under the authority of Saint Augustine, who regarded the canon as already closed and used the same list of twenty-seven books as supported by Athanasius, bishop of Alexandria, in AD 367. "Let this be made known ... for the purpose of confirming that Canon. Because we have received from our fathers that those books must be read in the Church."
Codex Canonum Ecclesiæ Africanæ

Council of Constantinople
May 5, 553 AD

One hundred sixty-five bishops under Pope Vigilius and Emperor Justinian I confirmed the decisions of the first four general councils.

---

1   *Wikipedia*: <u>Development of the Christian Biblical Canon</u>

What Are the Apocryphal Books?

The fourteen apocryphal books were written between 425 BC and AD 33 and were never a part of the canon of Scriptures which were accepted by the early church fathers. It was not until April 8, 1546, during the fourth session of the Council of Trent that the Catholic church officially accepted the apocryphal books as *deutero-canonical* or "second-degree" inspired. Protestants reject the idea of any kind of second-degree inspiration. The Apocrypha is made up of 14 books, with 173 chapters, 5,719 verses, and 155,875 words.[1]

Name of Books	Written	Chapters	Verses
Tobit	(250–175 BC)	14	244
Judith	(175–110 BC)	16	339
Additions to Esther	(180–145 BC)	7	108
1 Maccabees	(103–63 BC)	16	924
2 Maccabees	(c. 100 BC)	15	555
The Wisdom of Solomon	(150 BC–AD 40)	19	435
Ecclesiasticus	(190 BC)	51	1,391
1 Esdras	(c. 150 BC)	9	447
2 Esdras	(AD 70–135)	16	874
Baruch	(200 BC)	6	213
Prayer of Manasseh	(150–50 BC)	1	15
Song of the Three Young Men	(167 BC)	1	68
Susanna	(c. 100 BC)	1	64
Bel and the Dragon	(150–100 BC)	1	42
(Total)		173	5,719

---

1   Bruce Metzger, *The New Oxford Annotated Bible with the Apocrypha*.

There are an additional twenty-nine *apocryphal* books (spurious writings) and ninety-five more *pseudepigraphal* books (known forgeries) which were never admitted to the canon of Scripture by the early Christians for the following reasons[1]:

1. They were known as spurious or false. False names were used for authorship.

2. They were not a part of the Old Testament canon. The Jews never accepted them as the Word of God.

3. Jesus and His disciples knew of the apocryphal books but never once quoted from them, while the New Testament does quote the Old Testament 2,559 times.

4. There are no prophets associated with these writings. They do not claim to be the inspired word of God (2 Maccabees 2:23 and 15:38).

5. The apocryphal books were written during the silent era between Malachi, 425 BC, and the New Testament, AD 33. According to Malachi 3:1, the next and final prophet to appear before the coming of the Messiah would be John the Baptist.

6. Various credible ancient sources that frequently allude to and quote from the Old Testament exclude the apocryphal books from the canon.

   Philo (20 BC–AD 50)
   Josephus (AD 37–95)
   Melito (died AD 170)

7. The apocryphal and pseudepigraphal books contain many historical, geographical, and doctrinal errors.

---

1   Merrill Unger, *Unger's Bible Handbook*, p. 70.

What Is the Gospel of Barnabas?

There are two books called the Gospel of Barnabas. The <u>first</u>[1] is a thirteen-page letter written around AD 100 during the reign of Emperor Trajan (AD 97–117) or Hadrian (AD 117–138). It was not written by the Barnabas mentioned in the New Testament (Acts 4:36-37). It mentions the destruction of Jerusalem in AD 70. It quotes the Old Testament 110 times and the New Testament 15 times. It makes mention of the following Christian words and phrases:

Father (as God): 3 times
The Son of God: 10 times
The Holy Spirit: 12 times
Jesus: 15 times
Messiah: 3 times
The Lord Jesus Christ: 2 times
The crucifixion of Christ as an atonement: 11 times
Christ's resurrection from the dead: 2 times
Lord: 67 times
God: 31 times
Lord God: 7 times

The <u>second</u>[2] Gospel of Barnabas is a 366-page book with 222 chapters written in Italian in the Middle Ages around the fourteenth or fifteenth century by Fra Marino, a catholic priest who converted to Islam. The purpose of this book was to discredit Christianity. There are many historical, geographical, and internal contradictions within it. This second Middle-Ages Gospel of Barnabas conflicts with both the Bible and the Qur'an in numerous places as seen in the following examples.

---

1   Philip Schaff, *The Ante-Nicene Fathers*, Vol. 1, p. 133.
2   Lonsdale and Laura Ragg, *The Gospel of Barnabas*, 1907.

Problems Within the False Barnabas[1]

1. "Jesus went by boat from the Sea of Galilee to Nazareth (chapter 20). When Jesus came to Nazareth he boarded a boat ... and came to Jerusalem" (chapters 151-152). There are no lakes or rivers in this area!

2. Chapter 54 mentions 60 *minuti,* a gold dinar, which did not exist at the time of Jesus, but was used in the Middle Ages in Spain.

3. The 152nd chapter mentions "wooden wine kegs" being used to store wine, but these were unknown during the time of Jesus. These were not used until the Middle Ages. Leather wineskins were used at the time of Jesus (Matthew 9:17).

4. In the 222nd chapter, it quotes the Diatessaron, which was written during the thirteenth to fourteenth centuries. It also quotes Dante's (AD 1265–1321) poems. It also quotes from Jerome's Latin Vulgate, which was completed around AD 405. These quotations show that it could not be a first-century writing.

5. According to the false Barnabas (chapters 3 and 127), Pontius Pilate was the governor of Philistia at both Jesus' birth and death. However, Pilate did not begin his reign until AD 26.

6. According to the 93rd chapter, the high priest, Herod, and Pilate together bowed down in worship before Jesus' feet. This runs contrary to the Bible and the facts, as these men hated Jesus and would not have wanted to worship Him.

7. Barnabas denies that Jesus was the Messiah; however, both the Bible and the Qur'an affirm that Jesus was the Messiah (Daniel 9:24-26; Matthew 16:13-17; John 1:41, 4:25-26; Mâ'ide 5:17, 72; Al-i-İmran 3:45; Nisâ 4:157, 172; Tevbe 9:30-31).

8. According to the New Testament, the true Barnabas was a partner in the gospel with Paul (Acts 13:1-3, 43), but in chapter 222, the false Barnabas labels Paul's teachings as being false.

---

1   R. Benson, *İncîl-i Barnaba*, pp. 227-278.

Would the Unfaithfulness of the Jews Affect the Faithfulness of God to His Holy Books?

From the Bible

Jeremiah 31:35-37 – (35) Thus saith the Lord, which giveth the sun for a light by day, *and* the ordinances of the moon and of the stars for a light by night, which divideth the sea when the waves thereof roar; The Lord of hosts *is* his name: (36) If those ordinances depart from before me, saith the Lord, *then the seed of Israel also shall cease from being a nation before me for ever*. (37) Thus saith the Lord; If heaven above can be measured, and the foundations of the earth searched out beneath, I will also cast off all the seed of Israel for all that they have done, saith the Lord.

Jeremiah 51:5 – For Israel *hath* not *been* forsaken, nor Judah of his God, of the Lord of hosts; though their land was filled with sin against the Holy One of Israel.

Romans 3:1-4 – (1) What advantage then hath the Jew? or what profit is there of circumcision? (2) Much every way: chiefly, because that unto them were committed the oracles of God. (3) For what if some did not believe? shall their unbelief make the faith of God without effect? (4) God forbid: yea, let God be true, but every man a liar; as it is written, That thou mightiest be justified in thy sayings, and mightest overcome when thou art judged.

Romans 11:1-2 – (1) I say then, Hath God cast away his people? God forbid. For I also am an Israelite, of the seed of Abraham, *of* the tribe of Benjamin. (2) God hath not cast away his people which he foreknew.

From the Qur'an

Bakara 2:88-89 – (88) They (the Jews) say: "Our hearts are wrappings (which are enough to preserve the divine word)," but <u>Allah has cursed them for their unbelief</u> ... (89) And now that a Scripture from Allah confirming their own (the Torah) – though before they were asking for a victory over the disbelievers – has come <u>they deny it</u>, although they know it to be the truth. May <u>Allah's curse be on the disbelievers</u>.

Nisâ 4:46 – Some of those who are Jews <u>change words from their context and say</u>: "We hear and disobey; hear you as one who hears not"; and "<u>listen to us!</u>" <u>distorting with their tongues</u> and belittling religion.

Mâ'ide 5:12-15 – (12) Allah made a covenant of old with the Children of Israel ... (13) And <u>because of their breaking their covenant, We have cursed them</u> and made hard their hearts. <u>They change words from their context and forget a part</u> of that wherewith they had been reminded. You will not cease to discover treachery among them, all save a few. But bear with them, and pardon them. Surely, Allah loves those who are kind. (14) And with those who say: "Surely, we are Christians," We made a covenant, but <u>they forgot a part of that whereof they were admonished</u>. Therefore <u>we have stirred up enmity and hatred among them till the day of Resurrection</u>, when Allah will inform them of what they have done. (15) O people of the Scripture! Now has our messenger come, to you, expounding to you <u>much of what you used to hide in the Scripture</u>, and forgiving much. Now there has come to you light from Allah, and a plain scripture.

What Are the Real Reasons for the Muslim Claims of Corruption?

Muhammad was an illiterate Arab, an *ummi*, one who did not know how to read or write (A'raf 7:157-158). The Qur'an states that Muhammad had never read the Bible before he received the revelation of the Qur'an (Ankebut 29:48; Shu'ara 42:52). Muhammad thought that the revelation he was receiving was no different from what was written in the Bible (Fussilet 41:43). At first, Muhammad believed that Jews and Christians would confirm that what he was receiving would be compatible with the Bible (Fâtir 35:31). Because of this assumption, Muhammad's early suras, which were written during the Mecca period, were positive about the Jews and Christians (En'âm 6:20, 114, 154-157). Therefore, there are many suras written during the Meccan period (see p. 17) which praised the Jews and especially the Christians (İsra 17:107-108; Shu'ara 26:196-197). He even advised potential Muslims that they could verify what he was saying with the Jews and Christians if they had any doubt about what he was teaching (Yunus 10:94).

Muhammad had already repeatedly affirmed that the Bible was the Word of God, but as time passed, he was forced to recognize that there were many doctrinal contradictions between the Qur'an and the Bible. As Muhammad moved to Medina, and as more and more suras of the Qur'an were being written, Muhammad began to be severely criticized by both Jews and Christians for the many obvious contradictions between the Qur'an and the Bible (Bakara 2:88-89, 91, 111, 120, 145; Mâ'ide 5:64). Because Muslims had no other explanation for these obvious contradictions between the Bible and the Qur'an, to maintain credibility they were forced to make the claim that the Bible had been changed.

The Jews of Medina asked proof of Muhammad's claim to be a prophet, by producing either a miracle or a word of prophecy about the future. (En'âm 6:37-38, 124; A'raf 7:187-188). Muhammad admitted that he was unable to do any miracles and he was unable to give any prophecy about the future (Yunus 10:20; En'âm 6:50).

The Jews then accused Muhammad of being demon possessed (Tekvir 81:22-25). Muhammad's attitude towards Jews and Christians quickly changed during the Medina period, and his tone towards them became more critical, to the point where he began to advocate attacking and killing Jews and Christians as the enemies of Allah (Bakara 2:191-193; Al-i İmran 3:18-20; Tevbe 9:5, 29-30; Tegabun 64:14).

The Qur'an twice makes the claim that the Bible contains prophetic reference to the coming of Muhammad (A'raf 7:157; Saf 61:6). Many Muslim scholars have therefore tried to use a variety of Scriptures from the Bible to show a prophetic connection to Muhammad (see Genesis 16:3; 17:1-10, 19-20, 25-26; 25:13-16; 49:10; Deuteronomy 18:15, 18; 33:1-2; 34:12; 1 Kings 8:41-43; Psalm 45:3-5; 91:1-16; 149:1-9; Song of Solomon 5:10-16; Isaiah 21:6-7, 13-17; 28:9-13; 29:12; 33:15-19; 42:1-4, 11; 53:1-12; 63:1-6; Daniel 2:29; 7:13-14; Habakkuk 3:3; Zephaniah 3:9; Matthew 3:11; 21:43; Mark 1:7; John 1:21; 4:21; 14:16-17, 30; 15:26; 16:7, 13; Acts 3:22-26). However, a study of these passages in their context shows that not one of these verses really has anything to do with Muhammad. Therefore, Muslims have been forced to make an *a priori* assumption that Christians must have taken the verses about Muhammad out of the Bible.

Some Difficult Questions for Muslims to Consider

Who Changed the İnjil? In order for the İnjil to be changed, there must be a person or persons in church history who were responsible for plotting and carrying out this change. What are the names of these traitors to the faith and what would motivate them? Would God-fearing Christians stand by and let evil men get away with such a diabolical plan without a fight?

What books or parts of the İnjil were changed? Was the supposed corruption total or just partial? Which specific parts were affected? What percentage of the İnjil was changed? What are the criteria for determining which parts were changed? If the İnjil was corrupted, why does the Qur'an still affirm believing in and obeying it?

When was the İnjil changed? Was the so-called corruption of the İnjil before or after the time of Muhammad? If it was before Muhammad, then why does Muhammad affirm the İnjil of his day as the Word of God instead of saying that it was changed? If it was after Muhammad, then why do over 5,600 Greek manuscripts of the İnjil plus over 10,000 Latin manuscripts which pre-date İslam all say the same thing?

Where was the İnjil changed? In what city or location was this supposed corruption to have taken place? Was this supposed corruption a local phenomenon or was it worldwide? Where can we find the original İnjil and compare it with the present İnjil? Where is the original text of the İnjil if it was supposed to have been changed as is claimed?

Why was the *İnjil* changed? Why would any God-fearing Christian ever want to change the life-giving enlightenment of their own Holy Book? Why would any real Christian ever attempt to change the gospel of God when they knew that the penalty for such an action would be their own eternal damnation?

Why would Muslims not keep a copy of the original İnjil, which they claim has been changed, to show the specific differences between the original İnjil and the one that exists today?

How would all of the different sects and denominations of both the Jews and Christians ever arrive at complete agreement as to decide which changes should be made to the Bible? How would true Christians ever allow such a thing?

How could Christians possibly gather together all of the manuscripts of the New Testament to change them, when by AD 325, there were already churches with manuscripts of the İnjil scattered everywhere from as far away as India, Ethiopia, Turkey, Germany, and Ireland? How could Christians from all over the world suddenly make thousands of copies of the original İnjil disappear without a trace and then rewrite a new İnjil?

How would God still be almighty if He allowed Satan to exalt himself over God and thwart the purpose and power of God by corrupting God's Holy Books? Would God not want to stop Satan's scheme to change them? If God wanted to stop Satan from corrupting the Bible, then why didn't He?

How is it that Muslims cannot give the name of even one historian to document that the Bible has been changed? If the Bible had been seriously changed or compromised in AD 325, or at any other time in history, would not this important fact have been widely publicized at that time?

How can Muslims honestly say they believe Jesus is a prophet and yet not read or obey the very words of Jesus as they are recorded in the İnjil without themselves becoming a *Kafir* or unbeliever according to the Qur'an? How can Muslims think they are not being hypocritical while believing in the Qur'an but not in the same way believe the Bible, which they are commanded to believe in by the Qur'an itself? How can a Muslim think that God would have a double standard to protect the Qur'an but to not protect all of the other Holy Books in the same way?

Seven Reasons Why Christians Do Not Believe in the Qur'an

1. Muhammad was an illiterate Arab from the tribe of Quraish who was anti-Jewish, but according to the Bible, God chose to reveal His Holy Books only through the agency of the Jews. (A'raf 7:157-158)

> **Romans 3:1-2** – (1) <u>What advantage then hath the Jew?</u> or what profit is there of circumcision? (2) <u>Much every way</u>: chiefly, because <u>unto them were committed the oracles of God.</u>

> **Romans 9:4** – Who are <u>Israelites;</u> to whom pertaineth the adoption, and the glory, and <u>the covenants</u>, and the giving of <u>the law</u>, and the service of God, and <u>the promises.</u>

2. Muhammad's message was fundamentally in disagreement with the message of Jesus and the other the prophets of the Bible. (Nisâ 4:157)[1]

> **Isaiah 8:20** – To the law and to the testimony: <u>if they speak not according to this word</u>, it is because <u>there is no light in them.</u>

> **Galatians 1:8** – But though we, <u>or an angel from heaven</u>, preach <u>any other gospel</u> unto you than that which we have preached unto you, let <u>him be accursed.</u>

> **1 Corinthians 14:32-33** – (32) And <u>the spirits of the prophets are subject to the prophets.</u> (33) For <u>God is not the author of confusion,</u> but of peace.

3. Muhammad's self-proclamation as a prophet is not a valid criterion for prophethood, and there are no other valid proofs for his being a prophet.

> **John 5:31** – <u>If I bear witness of myself, my witness is not true.</u>

> **John 5:36** – for the works which the Father hath given me to finish, <u>the same works that I do, bear witness of me</u>, that the Father hath sent me.

4. Muhammad did not do any obvious miracles like Jesus and the other prophets did. (En'âm 6:37)

---

1   To compare the Holy Books, see Dan's website: <u>200 Questions About the Bible and the Quran</u>, *danwickwire.com.*

John 14:11 – Believe me that I am in the Father, and the Father in me: or else <u>believe me for the very works' sake.</u>

John 20:30-31 – (30) And <u>many other signs</u> truly did Jesus in the presence of his disciples, which are not written in this book: (31) <u>but these are written, that ye might believe that Jesus is the</u> Christ, the Son of God.

5. Muhammad did not have a spirit of prophecy like Jesus and the other prophets had. (En'âm 6:50)

1 Samuel 9:9 – (Beforetime in Israel, when a man went to enquire of God, thus he spake, Come, and let us go to <u>the seer</u>: for <u>he that is now called a Prophet was beforetime called a Seer.</u>)

Revelation 19:10 – Worship God: for <u>the testimony of Jesus is the spirit of prophecy.</u>

6. Muhammad claimed to be the last of the prophets, but God had already closed the canon of Scripture at the end of the book of Revelation. (Ahzab 33:40)

Revelation 22:18 – For I testify unto every man that heareth the words of the prophecy of this book, <u>If any man shall add unto these things, God shall add unto him the plagues</u> that are written in this book.

7. Muhammad taught doctrines which are diametrically opposed to the teachings of the Bible and which propagate the spirit of Antichrist. (Tevbe 9:30-31)

1 John 2:22 – Who is a liar but he that denieth that Jesus is the Christ? <u>He is antichrist, that denieth the Father and the Son.</u>

1 John 4:1-3 – (1) Beloved, <u>believe not every spirit</u>, but <u>try the spirits</u> whether they are of God: because many false prophets are gone out into the world. (2) Hereby know ye the Spirit of God: <u>Every spirit that confesseth that Jesus Christ is come in the flesh is of God</u>: (3) And <u>every spirit that confesseth not that Jesus Christ is come in the flesh is not of God</u>: <u>and this is that spirit of antichrist</u>, whereof ye have heard that it should come; and even now already is it in the world.

God's Eternal Plan of Salvation

God is holy, and commands us to be holy.
Leviticus 11:44-45 – (44) For <u>I am the LORD your God</u>: ye shall therefore sanctify yourselves, and ye shall be holy; for <u>I am holy</u>. (45) be holy, for I am holy.
Hebrews 12:14 – <u>Follow</u> peace with all men, and <u>holiness</u>, without which no man shall see the Lord.
1 Peter 1:15-16 – (15) But as he which hath called you is holy, so <u>be ye holy in all manner of conversation</u>; (16) because it is written, <u>Be ye holy; for I am holy</u>.

God's Holy Books define sin and condemn it.
Psalm 130:3 – <u>If thou, LORD, shouldest mark iniquities, O Lord, who shall stand</u>?
John 8:34 – <u>Whosoever committeth sin is the servant of sin</u>.
Romans 14:23 – <u>whatever is not of faith is sin</u>.
James 2:10 – For whosoever shall keep the whole law, and yet <u>offend in one point</u>, he is <u>guilty of all</u>.
James 4:17 – Therefore <u>to him that knoweth to do good, and doeth it not, to him it is sin</u>.
1 John 3:4 – Whosoever committeth sin transgresseth also the law: for <u>sin is the transgression of the law</u>.
1 John 5:17 – <u>All unrighteousness is sin</u>.

All people are sinful and guilty before a Holy God.
Jeremiah 13:23 – Can the Ethiopian change his skin, or the leopard his spots? <u>then may ye also do good, that are accustomed to do evil</u>.
Proverbs 20:9 – <u>Who can say, I have made my heart clean, I am pure from my sin</u>?
Ecclesiastes 7:20 – For <u>there is not a just man upon earth, that doeth good, and sinneth not</u>.
Romans 3:10, 23 – (10) As it is written, <u>There is none righteous, no, not one</u>. (23) for <u>all have sinned, and come short of the glory of God</u>.

The wages of sin is death.

Ezekiel 18:4 – <u>The soul that sinneth, it shall die</u>.

Jeremiah 31:30 – But <u>every one shall die for his own iniquity</u>.

Romans 6:23 – <u>For the wages of sin is death</u>; but the gift of God is eternal life through Jesus Christ our Lord.

James 1:15 – And <u>sin, when it is finished, bringeth forth death.</u>

Luke 12:5 – But I will forewarn you whom ye shall fear: <u>Fear him, which after he hath killed hath power to cast into hell</u>; yea, I say unto you, Fear him.

God's desire is to save His people.

2 Peter 3:9 – <u>The Lord</u> is not slack concerning his promise, as some men count slackness; but <u>is longsuffering to us-ward, not willing that any should perish</u>, but that all should come to repentance.

Romans 5:8 – But <u>God commendeth his love toward us,</u> in that, <u>while were yet sinners, Christ died for us</u>.

1 John 4:8-10 – (8) God is love. (9) <u>In this was manifested the love of God toward us</u>, because that God sent his only begotten Son into the world, that we might live through him. (10) Herein is love, not that we loved <u>God</u>, but that <u>he loved us</u>, and <u>sent his Son to be the propitiation for our sins</u>.

God has provided only one way for sinners to be saved.

John 14:6 – <u>Jesus</u> saith unto him, <u>I am the way</u>, the truth, and the life: no man cometh unto the Father, but by me.

John 17:3 – And <u>this is life eternal</u>, that they might <u>know thee the only true God</u>, and <u>Jesus Christ</u>, whom thou has sent.

Acts 4:10, 12 – (10) by the name of Jesus Christ ... (12) <u>Neither is there salvation in any other</u>: for there is <u>none other name</u> under heaven given among men, <u>whereby we must be saved</u>.

1 Timothy 2:5 – For there is one God, and <u>one mediator between God and men</u>, the man <u>Christ Jesus</u>.

God's provision for man to be saved from the punishment of sin has always involved the ransom of a blood sacrifice!

Leviticus 17:11 – For the life of the flesh is in <u>the blood</u>: and I have given it to you upon the altar <u>to make an atonement for your souls</u>: for <u>it is the blood that maketh an atonement for the soul</u>.

Matthew 20:28 – Even as <u>the Son of man came</u> not to be ministered unto, but to minister, and <u>to give his life a ransom for many</u>.

1 Corinthians 5:7 – For even <u>Christ</u> our Passover <u>is sacrificed for us</u>.

Hebrews 9:22 – And almost all things are by the law purged with blood; and <u>without shedding of blood is no remission</u>.

God gives people the freedom of choice as to whether or not they will choose to believe and obey His Holy Books.

Deuteronomy 11:26-28 – (26) Behold, <u>I set before you</u> this day a <u>blessing</u> and a <u>curse</u>; (27) a blessing, if ye obey the commandments of the LORD your God, (28) and a curse, if ye will not obey the commandments of the LORD your God.

Deuteronomy 30:19 – I have set before you life and death, blessing and cursing: therefore <u>choose life</u>.

Joshua 24:15 – And if it seem evil unto you to serve the LORD, <u>choose you this day whom ye will serve</u> ... <u>but as for me and my house, we will serve the LORD</u>.

God sent Jesus Christ, the Son of God, to die as the sacrificial atonement for the sin of the world.

Isaiah 53:5-6 – (5) But <u>he was wounded for our transgressions, he was bruised for our iniquities</u>: the chastisement of our peace was upon him; and with his stripes we are healed. (6) All we like sheep have gone astray; we have turned every one to his own way; and <u>the LORD hath laid on him the iniquity of us all</u>.

Matthew 26:27-28 – (27) And he [Jesus] took the cup, and gave thanks, and gave it to them, saying, Drink ye all of it;

(28) for <u>this is my blood</u> of the new testament, <u>which is shed</u> <u>for many for the remission of sins</u>.

John 1:29, 34 – (29) John seeth Jesus coming unto him, and saith, <u>Behold the Lamb of God, which taketh away the</u> <u>sin of the world</u>. (34) and I saw, and bare record that this is the Son of God.

1 Peter 1:18-20 – (18) Forasmuch as ye know that <u>ye were</u> not <u>redeemed</u> with corruptible things, ... (19) but <u>with the</u> <u>precious blood of Christ</u>, as of a lamb without blemish or spot: (20) who verily was foreordained.

1 Corinthians 15:1-4 – (1) Moreover, brethren, I declare unto you the gospel which I preached unto you, which also ye have received, and wherein ye stand; (2) by which also ye are saved, ... (3) <u>Christ died for our sins</u> according to the scriptures; (4) and that he was buried, and that <u>he arose</u> <u>again the third day</u> according to the scriptures.

Ephesians 1:7 – we have redemption <u>through his blood</u>, <u>the forgiveness of sins</u>, according to the riches of his grace.

Salvation does not come by our own good works, but it is a gift freely given by God.

Romans 3:28 – Therefore we conclude that <u>a man is justi-</u> <u>fied by faith without the deeds of the law</u>.

Romans 4:2 – For <u>if Abraham were justified by works</u>, he hath whereof to glory; but not before God.

Ephesians 2:8-9 – (8) <u>For by grace are ye saved through</u> <u>faith; and that not of yourselves: it is the gift of God: (9) not</u> <u>of works, lest any man should boast</u>.

Titus 3:4-6 – (4) But after that the kindness and love of God our Saviour toward man appeared, (5) <u>not by works of righ-</u> <u>teousness which we have done, but according to his mercy</u> <u>he saved us, by the washing of regeneration, and renewing</u> <u>of the Holy Ghost</u>; (6) which he shed on us abundantly through Jesus Christ our Saviour.

In order for a person to enter into the kingdom of heaven, they must be born again by God's Holy Spirit.

John 3:3, 5 – (3) Jesus answered and said unto him, Verily, verily, I say unto thee, <u>Except a man be born again, he cannot see the kingdom of God.</u> (5) Verily, verily, I say unto thee, <u>Except a man be born of water and of the Spirit, he cannot enter into the kingdom of God.</u>

2 Corinthians 5:17 – Therefore <u>if any man be in Christ, he is a new</u> creature: old things are passed away; behold, <u>all things are become new.</u>

1 Peter 1:23 – <u>Being born again,</u> not of corruptible seed, but of incorruptible, <u>by the word of God,</u> which liveth and abideth for ever.

Those who accept Jesus Christ as their Lord and Savior are promised that they will inherit eternal life.

John 3:36 – He that believeth on the Son <u>hath everlasting life.</u>

John 5:24 – <u>He that heareth my word,</u> and believeth on him that sent me, hath everlasting life.

John 6:47 – Verily, verily, I say unto you, <u>He that believeth on me hath everlasting life.</u>

John 11:25-26 – (25) Jesus said ... <u>I am the resurrection, and the life:</u> he that believeth in me, though he were dead, yet shall he live: (26) and whosoever liveth and believeth in me shall never die.

Those who reject Christ's substitutionary death on the cross as an atonement for their sin will have to pay their own penalty in hell.

John 3:18 – He that believeth on him is not condemned: but <u>he that believeth not is condemned already,</u> because he hath not believed in the name of the only begotten Son of God.

John 8:24 – I said therefore unto you, that <u>ye shall die in your sins:</u> for if ye believe not that I am he, <u>ye shall die in your sins.</u>

John 12:48 – He that rejecteth me, and receiveth not my words, hath one that judgeth him: the word that I have spoken, the same shall judge him in the last day.

God gives serious warnings about the consequence of rejecting the gift of salvation which He has freely provided.

2 Thessalonians 1:7-9 – (7) The Lord Jesus shall be revealed from heaven with his mighty angels, (8) in flaming fire taking vengeance on them that know not God, and that obey not the gospel of our Lord Jesus Christ: (9) who shall be punished with everlasting destruction from the presence of the Lord.

Hebrews 2:3 – How shall we escape, if we neglect so great salvation.

1 Peter 4:17-18 – (17) For the time is come that judgment must begin at the house of God: and if it first begin at us, what shall the end be of them that obey not the gospel of God? (18) And if the righteous scarcely be saved, where shall the ungodly and the sinner appear?

Those who accept Jesus as Lord and Savior should be baptized as a public declaration of their faith in Christ.

Matthew 28:18-20 – (18) And Jesus came and spake unto them, saying, All power is given unto me in heaven and in earth. (19) Go ye therefore, and teach all nations, baptizing them in the name of the Father, and of the Son, and the Holy Ghost: (20) teaching them to observe all things whatsoever I have commanded you.

Acts 2:38 – The Peter said unto them, Repent, and be baptized every one of you in the name of Jesus Christ for the remission of sins, and ye shall receive the gift of the Holy Ghost.

Blessing or Cursing:
The Choice Is Yours

Deuteronomy 28:1-2 – And it shall come to pass, <u>if thou shalt hearken diligently unto the voice of the LORD thy God, to observe and to do all his commandments</u> which I command thee this day, that the LORD thy God will set thee on high above all nations of the earth: And all these blessings shall come on thee, and overtake thee, <u>if thou shalt hearken unto the voice of the LORD thy God</u>.

Deuteronomy 28:6 – Blessed shalt thou be when thou comest in, and blessed shalt thou be when thou goest out.

Deuteronomy 28:13-19 – And the LORD shall make thee the head, and not the tail; and thou shalt be above only, and thou shalt not be beneath; <u>if that thou hearken unto the commandments of the LORD thy God</u>, which I command thee this day, <u>to observe and to do them</u>: And thou shalt not go aside from any of the words which I command thee this day, to the right hand, or to the left, to go after other gods to serve them. But it shall come to pass, <u>if thou wilt not hearken unto the voice of the LORD thy God, to observe to do</u> all his commandments and his statutes which I command thee this day; that all these curses shall come upon thee, and overtake thee: Cursed shalt thou be in the city, and cursed shalt thou be in the field. Cursed shall be thy basket and thy store. Cursed shall be the fruit of thy body, and the fruit of thy land, the increase of thy [cows], and the flocks of thy sheep. Cursed shalt thou be when thou comest in, and cursed shalt thou be when thou goest out.

Deuteronomy 30:19 – I call heaven and earth to record this day against you, that <u>I have set before you life and death, blessing</u> and <u>cursing</u>: therefore <u>choose life</u>, that both thou and thy seed may live.

God has set in motion certain universal principles which always work in the same manner for everyone, regardless of time, race, or religion. According to Deuteronomy chapter 28, there are two universal conditions for <u>blessing</u> and for <u>cursing</u>. The condition for being blessed is to <u>read</u> and <u>obey</u> the Bible. The condition for being cursed is to <u>not read</u> the Bible and to <u>not obey</u> it.

A person could not possibly obey something about which they know nothing about. So any person who has not read the Bible cannot possibly be in a position to obey it, because they don't yet know what it is that God expects them to do or not to do. Muslims who say they believe in the *Tevrat, Zebur,* and İnjil, but refuse to read these books, based on the presupposition that the Bible has been changed, have only deceived themselves, and keep themselves bound under a curse of spiritual ignorance. Faith cannot exist in a dark vacuum of spiritual ignorance. "Faith comes by hearing and hearing by the word of God" (Romans 10:17). Any person's faith in order to be genuine and valid must be based upon the true and unchangeable facts of the Word of God.

Even according to the Qur'an, 90 percent of the content of the books which Muslims are required to believe in (that is, the *Tevrat, Zebur, İnjil,* and Qur'an) are found in the Bible! Muslims who have swallowed the lie that the Bible has been changed have unwittingly put their lives under the curse of being in bondage to the darkness of spiritual ignorance. Therefore, knowing the truths contained in this book and embracing them constitutes the very first and necessary step for a Muslim to walk in the light. This is the first step in the right direction towards a person's getting out from under a curse and getting under God's blessing!

Index of Bible Verses

Genesis 17:7	22	Psalm 103:8, 17-18	56
Genesis 17:19-20	22	Psalm 105:7-8, 10	18
Genesis 22:14	56	Psalm 111:7-8	14
Leviticus 11:44-45	88	Psalm 119:9, 105	49
Leviticus 17:11	90	Psalm 119:89-90	22, 52
Deuteronomy 4:2	38, 45	Psalm 119:105	55
Deuteronomy 7:9	22, 57	Psalm 119:130, 160	57
Deuteronomy 11:26-28	90	Psalm 119:142, 144	55
Deuteronomy 12:32	38	Psalm 119:152	14
Deuteronomy 28:1-2	94	Psalm 119:160	14, 22
Deuteronomy 28:6	94	Psalm 121:7-8	53
Deuteronomy 28:13-19	94	Psalm 130:3	88
Deuteronomy 29:29	22	Psalm 145:8-9	56
Deuteronomy 30:19	90, 94	Psalm 146:5-6	40
Deuteronomy 32:39	58	Proverbs 2:8	47
Joshua 24:15	90	Proverbs 20:9	88
Nehemiah 9:6	52	Ecclesiastes 7:20	88
1 Samuel 2:9-10	51	Isaiah 1:24	59
1 Samuel 9:9	4, 87	Isaiah 8:20	86
2 Samuel 7:24-25	23	Isaiah 14:24, 27	38, 50
1 Chronicles 29:11	58	Isaiah 40:8	23, 44
2 Chronicles 16:9	59	Isaiah 40:25-26	49
Job 33:12	50	Isaiah 46:9-11	40, 47
Psalm 12:6-7	40, 53	Isaiah 53:5-12	72, 90
Psalm 24:8, 10	51	Isaiah 54:10	57
Psalm 25:9, 14	53	Isaiah 55:11	23, 40, 45
Psalm 33:9-11	58	Isaiah 57:15	50
Psalm 33:11	14	Jeremiah 13:23	88
Psalm 48:14	49	Jeremiah 31:3, 31, 34	48
Psalm 73:24	53	Jeremiah 31:30	89
Psalm 89:31	22	Jeremiah 31:35-37	80
Psalm 89:34	18, 22	Jeremiah 36:27-28	38
Psalm 94:7-9	46	Jeremiah 51:5	80
Psalm 96:13	54	Ezekiel 18:4	89

Malachi 3:6......................................18
Matthew 1:18-21...........................72
Matthew 3:2....................................60
Matthew 5:17-18 ....18, 23, 45
Matthew 16:16-20.........................72
Matthew 20:28................................90
Matthew 24:35.........................23, 44
Matthew 26:27-28 90
Matthew 28:18-20 ....14, 93
Mark 2:5-11....................................72
Mark 12:24.....................................40
Mark 13:31...............................40, 45
Mark 14:61-62...............................72
Luke 12:5..89
Luke 16:17...............................18, 40
Luke 21:33......................................14
John 1:1-14.....................................72
John 1:29, 34..................................91
John 3:3, 5......................................92
John 3:18..92
John 3:36..92
John 4:25-26...................................72
John 4:29..4
John 5:24..92
John 5:31..86
John 5:36..86
John 6:47..92
John 8:24..92
John 8:34..88
John 11:25-26.................................92
John 12:48.......................38, 54, 93
John 14:6..89
John 14:11......................................87
John 17:3..89
John 20:28-29................................72
John 20:30-31..........................72, 87
Acts 2:22..9
Acts 2:38..93

Acts 4:10, 12..................................89
Romans 3:1-2.................................86
Romans 3:1-4.................................80
Romans 3:10, 23............................88
Romans 3:28...................................91
Romans 4:2.....................................91
Romans 5:8.....................................89
Romans 6:23...................................89
Romans 9:4.....................................86
Romans 11:1-2................................80
Romans 14:23.................................88
1 Corinthians 5:7...........................90
1 Corinthians 14:32-33..................86
1 Corinthians 14:37-38..........12, 44
1 Corinthians 15:1-4......................91
2 Corinthians 5:17..........................92
Galatians 1:8..................................86
Galatians 1:11-12...........................12
Ephesians 1:7.................................91
Ephesians 2:8-9..............................91
Philippians 2:5-11..........................72
Philippians 4:19.............................48
Colossians 1:15-22.........................72
1 Thessalonians 2:13........................8
2 Thessalonians 1:7-9.....................93
1 Timothy 2:5...........................72, 89
1 Timothy 4:15-16..........................73
2 Timothy 2:15...............................55
2 Timothy 3:14-17..........................12
2 Timothy 3:16-17..........................54
Titus 1:2...52
Titus 3:4-6......................................91
Hebrews 2:3....................................93
Hebrews 4:12-13...............9, 14, 46
Hebrews 4:14-15............................72
Hebrews 9:22..................................90
Hebrews 12:14................................88
Hebrews 13:8...........................14, 72

James 1:15 89
James 1:17 18
James 2:10 88
James 4:17 88
1 Peter 1:15-16 88
1 Peter 1:18-20 91
1 Peter 1:23 92
1 Peter 1:23, 25 .... 14, 23, 44
1 Peter 4:17-18 93
2 Peter 1:20-21 12
2 Peter 3:9 89
1 John 2:22 87

1 John 3:4 88
1 John 4:1-3 87
1 John 4:6, 8, 16 48
1 John 4:8-10 89
1 John 4:14-15 72
1 John 5:17 88
Revelation 1:1-3 12
Revelation 14:6 23
Revelation 19:10 .... 4, 87
Revelation 22:18 87
Revelation 22:19 38

Index of Qur'anic Verses

Fatih 1:1-2, 5 57
Bakara 2:20 .... 41, 50
Bakara 2:41, 91 30
Bakara 2:40, 44, 113 30
Bakara 2:42, 159, 174 36
Bakara 2:61, 85 31
Bakara 2:62 .... 26, 34
Bakara 2:75 .... 20, 37
Bakara 2:78 36
Bakara 2:85, 121 .... 26, 28, 37
Bakara 2:87 73
Bakara 2:88-89 81
Bakara 2:100 37
Bakara 2:106 19
Bakara 2:136 .... 16, 26, 61
Bakara 2:143 56
Bakara 2:213 31
Bakara 2:231 46
Bakara 2:253 73
Bakara 2:255 .... 41, 50, 58
Bakara 2:256 43
Bakara 2:285 26
Al-i İmran 3:3 .... 16, 73
Al-i İmran 3:3-4 .... 28, 31
Al-i İmran 3:48-50 31
Al-i İmran 3:7-9 57
Al-i İmran 3:9, 94 52
Al-i İmran 3:19 31
Al-i İmran 3:23 .... 31, 37
Al-i İmran 3:39 15
Al-i İmran 3:45-46, 55 .... 15, 73
Al-i İmran 3:47 73
Al-i İmran 3:49 73
Al-i İmran 3:55-56 .... 28, 34, 55, 73

Al-i İmran 3:66 36
Al-i İmran 3:71 36
Al-i İmran 3:84 26
Al-i İmran 3:78 .... 20, 37
Al-i İmran 3:79, 93-94 30
Al-i İmran 3:98 .... 31, 37
Al-i İmran 3:99 37
Al-i İmran 3:113-114 34
Al-i İmran 3:119 16
Al-i İmran 3:187 36
Al-i İmran 3:199 .... 27, 34
Nisâ 4:44 36
Nisâ 4:46 .... 20, 37, 81
Nisâ 4:47 30
Nisâ 4:85 56
Nisâ 4:136 .... 16, 44
Nisâ 4:150-151 .... 27, 28, 31 37
Nisâ 4:159 73
Nisâ 4:162 .... 27, 34
Nisâ 4:171 15
Nisâ 4:172 73
Mâ'ide 5:10-12 29
Mâ'ide 5:12-15 81
Mâ'ide 5:13 .... 20, 36, 37
Mâ'ide 5:15 36
Mâ'ide 5:41 20
Mâ'ide 5:42 37
Mâ'ide 5:43 30
Mâ'ide 5:44 .... 30, 36
Mâ'ide 5:45 30
Mâ'ide 5:46 .... 16, 31
Mâ'ide 5:47 54
Mâ'ide 5:48 31
Mâ'ide 5:61 36

Mâ'ide 5:62......................................37
Mâ'ide 5:66, 69 ....27, 34
Mâ'ide 5:68...............................16, 37
Mâ'ide 5:75......................................73
Mâ'ide 5:110....................................73
Mâ'ide 5:116-117............................47
En'âm 6:34 24
En'âm 6:50 5
En'âm 6:91.........................21, 36, 37
En'âm 6:93.......................................61
En'âm 6:114...............................41, 54
En'âm 6:115....................... 24, 41, 54
En'âm 6:157.....................................29
A'raf 7:157....................................21, 30
A'raf 7:159.......................................35
A'raf 7:162....................................21, 37
A'raf 7:169.................................30, 35
A'raf 7:188...5
A'raf 7:196.................................39, 52
Enfal 8:52..59
Tevbe 9:9...36
Tevbe 9:30-31.................................87
Tevbe 9:111 ....16, 52, 61
Yunus 10:17.....................................61
Yunus 10:64......................... 24, 44
Yunus 10:94-95..............................30
Hûd 11:57..................................39, 47
Yusuf 12:111 31
Ra'd 13:36..................................31, 37
Ra'd 13:39..19
İbrahim 14:47 24
Hijr 15:9.................25, 39, 41, 45, 61
Nahl 16:43 ....25, 30
Nahl 16:101.....................................19
İsra 17:55...16
İsra 17:66...56
İsra 17:77..................................24, 45
İsra 17:86...19

İsra 17:101 30
Kehf 18:17, 23-24 49
Kehf 18:27................................ 24, 44
Kehf 18:45.......................................51
Meryem 19:19 73
Meryem 19:21 73
Meryem 19:30 73
Meryem 19:31 73
Meryem 19:34 73
Ta-Ha 20:133..................................30
Enbiyâ 21:7 ....25, 30
Enbiyâ 21:10 ....25, 30
Enbiyâ 21:48....................................25
Enbiyâ 21:105 ....25, 30
Hajj 22:47, 52..................24, 41, 58
Hajj 22:54 53
Hajj 22:62.......................................50
Hajj 22:74.......................................59
Nur 24:35...55
Kasas 28:48-49...............................30
Ankebut 29:46-47 .... 16, 29
Lokman 31:27 41
Sejde 32:23......................................17
Ahzab 33:40 87
Ahzab 33:62 24
Sebe' 34:31, 38.......................... 29, 31
Fâtir 35:43..24
Sad 38:9, 35.....................................57
Mu'min 40:53-54.....................25, 35
Mu'min 40:56..................................46
Mu'min 40:69-70............................31
Fussilat 41:43 17
Shu'ara 42:14 31
Shu'ara 42:15 .... 17, 27
Zuhruf 43:4......................................15
Zuhruf 43:45-46..............................30
Zuhruf 43:61, 63 .... 17, 73
Jathiya 45:16, 31, 34.............29, 31, 35

Ahkâf 46:9 5	Hashr 59:23 .... 39, 51, 52, 53, 59
Ahkâf 46:12 .... 17, 30, 31	Saf 61:6-7 21
Muhammad 47:11 39	Jumu'ah 62:1 49
Muhammad 47:32 .... 39, 59	Jumu'ah 62:5 31
Fetih 48:23 25	Tahrîm 66:12 73
Kaf 50:29 .... 25, 44	Hakka 69:44-47 .... 24, 39, 41, 45, 51
Tur 51:58 48	Hakka 69:2, 51 55
Kamer 54:42 51	Jinn 72:26-28 .... 39, 47
Hadîd 57:22 15	Buruj 85:14, 21-22 48
Hadîd 57:27 17	Buruj 85:21-22 .... 41, 61
Mujâdila 58:10 .... 39, 41	Bayyina 98:4 31

Index of Foreign Words Used

A priori: Something assumed beforehand without examination.

Apocrypha: The fourteen spurious writings accepted by Catholics but rejected by Protestants.

Argumentum ad baculum: An appeal to the big stick! Might makes right.

Argumentum ad hominem: An appeal based on the character of the person against whom it is directed.

Argumentum ad ignorantium: An argument based on ignorance of the facts.

Argumentum ad populum: An argument based on popular feelings, passions, or prejudices, not the facts.

Argumentum ad verecundiam: An argument based on the reverence which most people feel for a great name without considering the evidence of the facts.

Argumentum non sequitur: The fallacy of the consequent occurs when the conclusion doesn't really follow from the premises by which it is supposed to be supported.

Deutero-canonical: Books which were accepted as second-degree inspired by the Catholic church.

el-Adl: The Just and Righteous One.

el-Alîm: The Omniscient One.

el-Azim: The Great and Mighty One.

el-Azîz: The Mighty One.

el-Bâsîr: The Observant One.

el-Hâdî: The Guide.

el-Hakem: The Judge.

el-Hakk: The Truth.

el-Hafîz: The Guardian.

el-Kadir: God-Almighty, the All-Powerful One.

el-Kavi: The Strong and Powerful One.

el-Jebbar: The All-Powerful One.

el-Kahhar: The Dominator.

el-Kebir: The Great One.

el-Kuddûs: The Most Holy One.

el-Mukît: The Provider.

el-Muktedir: The Prevailer.

el-Müheymin: The Preserver.

el-Mü'min: The Faithful One.

el-Nûr: The Light.

er-Rahîm: The Compassionate.

er-Rahmân: The Merciful.

er-Rakîb: The Watcher.

er-Reshîd: The Guide.

er-Rezzâk: The Supplier.

el-Vedûd: The Loving One.

el-Vehhâb: The Liberal Giver.

el-Velî: The Guardian.

Esmaül-Hüsna: The ninety-nine names of God, the most beautiful names. (Twenty-eight of these are listed above.)

Grammateis: Copyists. People who copied the books of the Old Testament.

Haşa!: God Forbid!

Hijrah: The migration or journey of the Islamic prophet Muhammad and his followers from Mecca to Yathrib, later renamed Medina by him, in the year CE 622.

Ignoratio Elenchi: An irrelevant conclusion arrived at by substituting some other proposition more or less closely related to it.

İnjil: The four Gospels, and also used for all twenty-seven books of the New Testament.

Jahiliyah: A people who are ignorant, or a period of ignorance.

Kâfir: An unbeliever. *Kâfirler*: unbelievers.

Kalimulla: The word, used of the Word of God. Also used of Jesus.

Kethubim: The thirteen poetical books of the Old Testament.

Lectionaries: A *lectionary* is a book or listing that contains a collection of Scripture readings appointed for Christian or Judaic worship on a given day or occasion.

Lengua-franca: The primary language spoken throughout an area.

Levh-i Mahfuz: The book, or Mother of the Book, used of the eternal Word of God.

Logos: The Word, referring to the Word of God.

Mensuh: The law of abrogation within Islam.

Miniscules: Minuscule script; a group of writing styles in ancient and medieval Greek or Latin manuscripts.

Minuti: A gold dinar, which did not exist at the time of Jesus, but was used in the Middle Ages in Spain.

Nebi: A prophet.

Nebi'im: The twenty-one prophetic books of the Old Testament.

Nesih: The law of abrogation within Islam.

Parashah: A section of the text.

Papyrus: Refers to a thick, paper-like material made from the pith of the papyrus plant, Cyperus papyrus. Papyrus can also refer to a document written on sheets of papyrus joined together side by side and rolled up into a scroll, an early form of a book.

Petitio principii: Arriving at a conclusion based on circular reasoning.

Pseudepigrapha: Known forgeries or writings with false authorship.

Sopherim: A class of Jews who copied the Old Testament.

Tanakh: The Old Testament books.

Torah: The five Books of Moses in the Old Testament.

Ummi: One who does not know how to read or write.

Uncials: Uncial is a majuscule script (written entirely in capital letters) commonly used from the fourth to eighth centuries AD by Latin and Greek scribes.

Zindiq: A hypocrite.

Bibliography

Atay, Hüseyin. *Kur'ân'a Göre Araştırmalar - I*. Ankara, Semih Ofset, 1993.

Benson, R. *İncîl-i Barnaba: Bilimsel Bir Araştırma*. İstanbul: 1985.

Bruce, F. F. *The New Testament Documents: Are They Reliable?* Downers Grove, Illinois: InterVarsity Press, 1964.

Bruce, F. F. *The Canon of Scripture*. Downers Grove, Illinois: InterVarsity Press, 1988.

Chafer, Lewis Sperry. *Systematic Theology*, 8 Vols., Dallas, Texas: Dallas Seminary Press, 1974.

Copi, İrving M., and Carl Cohen. *Introduction to Logic*. New York: Macmillan Publishing Company, 1990.

Coxe, A. Cleveland, ed. *The Ante-Nicene Fathers*, 10 Vols., Grand Rapids, Mich.: William B. Eerdmans Publishing Company, 1979.

Dake, Finis Jennings. *Dake Annotated Reference Bible*. Lawrenceville, Georgia: Dake Publishing, 1981.

Davidson, Samuel. *The Hebrew Text of the Old Testament*. London: Samuel Bagster & Sons, 1859.

Gairdner, W. H. T., and S. Abdul-Ahad. *The Gospel of Barnabas - An Essay and Enquiry*. Hyderabad, India, Henry Martyn Institute of Islamic Studies, 1975.

Geisler, Norman L., and William E. Nix. *A General Introduction to the Bible*. Chicago, Moody Press, 1968.

Gazzâlî, İmam-ı. *Esmâ'ül Hüsnâ Şerhi*. Mütercim: M. Ferşat, İstanbul, Merve Basım Yayın, 1968.

Gilchrist, John. *Origins and Sources of the Gospel of Barnabas*. Durban, South Africa, Jesus to the Muslims, 1980.

Hahn, Ernest. *The Integrity of the Bible According to the Qur'an and the Hadith*. Mississauga, Canada: Philoxenia, 1993.

Harris, R. Laird. *Inspiration and Canonicity of the Bible*. Grand Rapids, Mich.: Zondervan Publishing House, 1957.

Higab, Muhammad. *God's Attributes*. Cario, Darel-Manar for Publication, 1995.

Hill, Andrew E. *Baker's Handbook of Bible Lists*. Grand Rapids, Mich.: Baker Book House, 1981.

House, H. Wayne. *Chronological and Background Charts of the New Testament*. Grand Rapids, Mich.:1982.

Jeffery, Grant R. *The Signature of God: Astonishing Biblical Discoveries*. Toronto, Ontario: Frontier Research Publications, 1997.

Keskioğlu, Osman. *Nûzulünden İtibaren Kur'an-ı Kerim*. Ankara: Türkiye Diyanet Vakfı Yayınları, 1989.

Ibn İsma'il, Adan. *The Belief of Isma'il*, 2003.

McDowell, Josh. *Evidence That Demands a Verdict: Historical Evidences for the Christian Faith.* Arrowhead Springs, California: Campus Crusade for Christ International, 1972.

McDowell, Josh, and Bill Wilson, comp. *The Best of Josh McDowell: A Ready Defense.* Nashville: Thomas Nelson Publishers, 1993.

McDowell, Josh. *The New Evidence That Demands a Verdict.* Authentic Media, 1999.

Metzger, Bruce M., ed. *The New Oxford Annotated Bible with the Apocrypha*, Revised Standard Version, Expanded Edition. New York: Oxford University Press, 1977.

Metzger, Bruce M. *The Text of the New Testament.* New York: Oxford University Press, 1968.

Noyan, Bedri. *Anadilimizle Manzum Türkçe Kur'an-ı Kerim.* Ankara: Ayyıldız Yayınları, 1991.

Pache, René. *The Inspiration and Authority of Scripture.* Chicago: Moody Press, 1969.

Pfander, C. G. *The Mîzânu'l Haqq: Balance of Truth.* W. St. Clair Tisdall, London: Religious Tract Society, 1910.

Ragg, Lonsdale, and Laura Ragg. *The Gospel of Barnabas.* Oxford, England: Clarendon Press, 1907.

Ramm, Bernard. *Protestant Christian Evidences.* Chicago: Moody Press, 1957.

Robinson, John. "Redating the New Testament," 1976, *www.scborromeo.org.*

Seale, Morris S. *Muslim Theology: A Study of Origins with Reference to the Church Fathers.* London: Luzac and Company Limited, 1964.

Slick, Matthew J., *When Was the Bible Written and Who Wrote it?* Christian Apologetics & Research Ministry, *www.carm.org.*

Surburg, Raymond F. *How Dependable is the Bible?* Philadelphia: J. B. Lippincott Company, 1972.

Tatlısu, Ali Osman. *Esmâü'l-Hüsnâ Şerhi.* İstanbul, Seha Neşriyat, 1993.

Thieme, R. B. Jr. *Canonicity.* Houston, Texas: Berachah Publications, 1973.

Unger, Merrill F. *Unger's Bible Handbook.* Chicago: Moody Press, 1967.

Unger, Merrill F. *Unger's Guide to the Bible.* Wheaton, Illinois: Tyndale House Publishers, 1974.

Walton, Robert Cliffort. *Chronological and Background Charts of Church History.* Grand Rapids: Zondervan Publishing House, 1986.

Walton, Robert Cliffort. *Chronological and Background Charts of the Old Testament.* Grand Rapids: Zondervan Publishing House, 1978.

Westcott, B. F., and F. J .A. Hort. *The New Testament in the Original Greek.* Cambridge: Macmillan, 1882.

Zwemer, Samuel M. *The Moslem Doctrine of God: An Essay on the Character and Attributes of Allah According to the Koran and Orthodox Tradition.* New York: American Tract Society, 1905.

Meet the Author

Dan Wickwire was born in California in 1951 and grew up in the city of Bakersfield. His military service included three years in the U.S. army, during which he was trained as a medic, a paratrooper, and a Green Beret. He served a tour of duty as a combat medic in Vietnam.

Dan's education includes:

- Bakersfield College, earning an associate's degree in liberal arts.
- Multnomah School of the Bible, studying Bible, Hebrew, and Greek, and earning a bachelor's degree in theology.
- Columbia Graduate School of Bible & Missions, earning a master's degree in Bible.
- Summer Institute of Linguistics (SIL); University of Washington at Seattle; University of Texas at Arlington; and University of Oklahoma at Norman, studying linguistics. Dan earned a master's degree in linguistics at Pacific Western University.
- Ankara University in Ankara, Turkey, completing one year of doctoral studies in Islamics in the Department of Islamic Theology.

Dan is married to Devri and is the father of three sons: Derek Yekta, Andrew Nadir, and Peter Can. He is an ordained minister who served as a church planting missionary in Turkey for twenty-eight years. Dan and Devri currently reside in the Turkish Republic of Northern Cyprus.

Dan's books can be downloaded at:

danwickwire.com

* *100 Questions About the Bible and the Qur'an*, (in Turkish) 144 pages, 1st Ed. 2001, 2nd Ed. 2003; (in English) 1st Ed. 2003, 2nd Ed. 2004.

* *200 Questions About the Bible and the Qur'an*, 120 pages, 2014. Also available in: Albanian, Arabic, Azeri, Chinese, Dutch, English, Farsi, French, German, Kazak, Korean, Norwegian, Polish, Portuguese, Romanian, Russian, Spanish, and Turkish.

* *An Analytical Analysis of the Similarities and Differences Between the Qur'an and the Bible*, (in Turkish) 216 pages, 2007; (in English) 224 pages, 2007.

* *An Outline of Jihad in Islamic History*, 144 pages, 2015.

* *A Theological Sourcebook*, (in English) 240 pages, 1985; (in Turkish) 240 pages, 1987.

* *Has the Bible Been Changed?* (in Turkish) 48 pages, 1st Ed. 1987; 2nd Ed. 1994; 3rd Ed. 2007; 4th Ed. 2014; (in English) 96 pages, 1st Ed: 1987; 2nd Ed. 2007; 3rd Ed. 2011; 108 pages, 4th Ed. 2014.

* *The Reliability of the Scriptures According to Jewish, Christian and Islamic Sources*, (in Turkish only) 420 pages, 1999.

* *The Role of Prayer and Fasting in Binding and Loosing with Special Reference to the Problem of Reaching the Unreached People of the World Today*, unpublished thesis at Columbia, 78 pages, 1983.

* *The Sevmek Thesis: A Grammatical Analysis of the Turkish Verb System: Illustrated by the verb "Sevmek" = "To Love,"* published thesis (in English and Turkish), 170 pages, 1987; 2nd Ed. 1,000 pages, 2012.

* *The Wickwire Compendium of Islam*, 1,000 pages, 2010.

Made in the USA
San Bernardino, CA
03 March 2018